Robert Stacy-Judd

Maya Architecture
and the Creation
of a New Style

Robert Stacy-Judd

MAYA ARCHITECTURE AND THE CREATION OF A NEW STYLE

Text by David Gebhard
Photography by Anthony Peres

CAPRA PRESS
SANTA BARBARA
1993

*Special thanks to Constance Fearing
for her support and enthusiasm.*

Text copyright © 1993 by David Gebhard
Photographs copyright © by Anthony Peres
pages 50 - 58, 92, 93, 94, 96, 99, 111, front and back covers.
All rights reserved.
Printed in the United States of America.

Design by Rave Associates and Anthony Peres.
Scanning and film by In-Color, Santa Barbara.
Illustrations from the University of California, Santa Barbara.

LIBRARY OF CONGRESS CATALOGING-IN-PUBLICATION DATA
Gebhard, David.
Robert Stacy Judd : Maya architecture. the creation of a new style / David Gebhard.
p.   cm.

Includes bibliographical references and index.
ISBN 0-88496-351-9 : $30.00
1. Stacy-Judd, Robert – Criticism and interpretation.
2. Mayas – Architecture – Influence.   I. Title
NA737.S625G43   1993
720'.92—dc20   92-45278

CIP

CAPRA ❦ PRESS
Box 2068, Santa Barbara, California 93120

Table of Contents

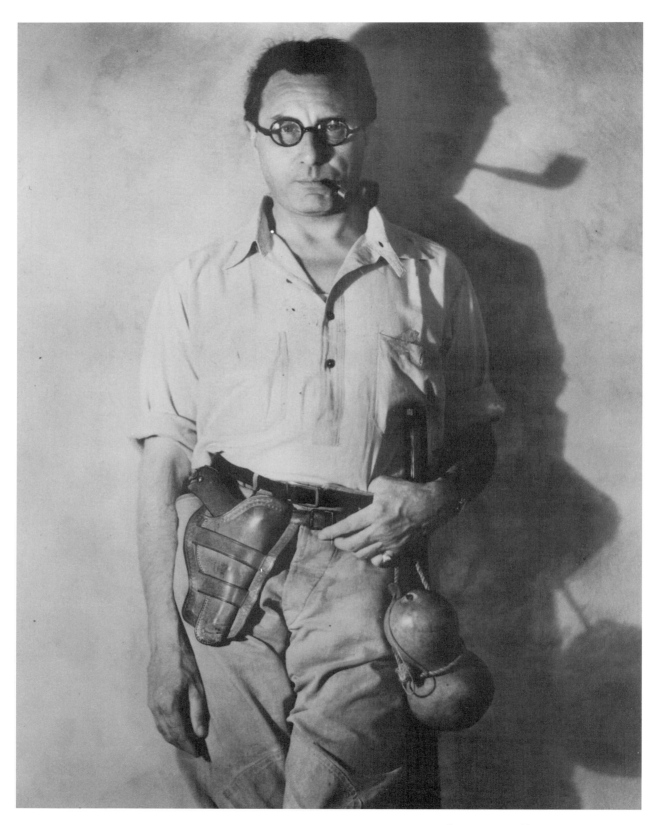

Robert B. Stacy-Judd, 1932.

Robert B. Stacy-Judd

IN LATE 1925, A SMALL TOURIST HOTEL opened near Los Angeles in the San Gabriel foothill town of Monrovia. The design of this hotel almost immediately attracted national and shortly international attention. In the May 14, 1925 issue of the *Los Angeles Evening Express* Will C. Davis commented "I cannot begin to describe it to you."[1] The reason for his oblique comment was the style of the hotel, which was based upon the pre-Columbian architecture of the Maya. An editorial in *The New York Times* noted that "The first building to be completed in the Maya style in the United States was finished in 1924 [sic]. It was the Aztec Hotel at Monrovia, near Los Angeles."[2] The editorial went on to reiterate a theme that continually cropped up in discussions of the revival of Mayan architecture in the 1920s and 1930s, "Out of it may be developed a new style which will be in every sense of the word indigenous in the New World."[3] This view was echoed in the pages of other newspapers nationwide, the *Christian Science Monitor,* the *Los Angeles Times,* and others.[4]

THE ALMOST INSTANT NOTORIETY (both pro and con) of this building was not only the result of its exotic "All-American" source of design, but even more because of its flamboyant architect, Robert B. Stacy-Judd. Though Stacy-Judd had only been in Southern California for a few years when he designed the hotel, he had quickly adapted himself to what was thought of then and now as the "mad" self-advertising quality of the place, a quality already associated with the Hollywood motion picture industry. Acting as his own publicity agent, Stacy-Judd held numerous interviews and penned letters and press releases which created the illusion that the Aztec Hotel was indeed the first example of the pre-Columbian revival in this country. He implied that he had spent several years "in a study of all available data before he turned over the design," when in fact his decision to employ Mayan motifs had only been arrived at a few weeks before he designed the building.[5] Like many other public relations artists he maneuvered the facts to form the self-aggrandized tale that he wished others to believe in (and as so often happens in the process he became a convert to it himself).

BY THE EARLY 1930s, he had managed to build only a small handful of modern Mayan adaptations, but he made the most of them to advertise himself and his architecture. As with the Aztec Hotel, these buildings were extensively published and republished in the popular as well as the professional architectural press, home shelter magazines and trade journals. After completion of the Aztec Hotel, he went on to

Chapter 1

write and publish a wide array of articles and present illustrated lectures that argued that a return to the architecture of the Maya was the only logical course for a modern American architecture of the twentieth century. He reinforced his authority by transforming himself into the personage of a romantic explorer/archaeologist who penetrated the dangerous jungles of Yucatan to "explore the mysteries of the Mayan pyramid."[6] From the date of his trip to Yucatan in 1930, he was fond of seeing himself portrayed in photographs as the classic, pith-helmeted, bold, macho explorer. Even as late as 1944, while working on the design for Howard Hughes's Spruce Goose, he selected a photograph of himself as the pith-helmeted explorer to be used in the company publication, and he was still stating that he was the "first architect to utilize Mayan architectural motifs under modern conditions."[7]

ON THE SURFACE STACY-JUDD'S emergence as an extravagant Hollywood-type personality in the twenties would seem to be a radical conversion for him since he was the product of a conservative British household, was educated at traditional English and Scottish schools, received his architectural education in the British Isles, and initially established his architectural practice there. Yet, even a brief look into his pre-1922 life pointedly illustrates that the picturesqueness of his personality and professional life was firmly established long before he arrived in America and Hollywood.

Childhood in England

ROBERT B. STACY-JUDD WAS BORN ON JUNE 21, 1884 into an upper-middle-class family who lived in the West End of London. The family home was "within a stone's throw of Buckingham Palace, the foreign diplomatic center and Rotten Row."[8] Both his father Benjamin Stacy-Judd and his mother Elizabeth Thompson Stacy-Judd were natives of London. The records indicate that his father, whose ancestry was Scottish, was a licensed victualer.

IN HIS UNPUBLISHED AUTOBIOGRAPHY, Stacy-Judd mentions that "due to the nature of my father's business my younger and only brother and I were left considerably to the care of strangers in numerous widely scattered centers. How many step-homes we occupied between birth and the time we rejoined our parents, I cannot remember."[9] Characteristic of the cultivated mysteries which Stacy-Judd created about his life, nowhere in his autobiography does he tell what his father's occupation was in order to explain his absences, nor does he provide any sense of how his mother responded to what was a rigorous male-dominated Victorian household.[10]

"DURING THAT PERIOD [OF CHILDHOOD] we were brought up in a rigid nineteenth-century discipline. A curriculum for behavior included exact hours for rising, retiring, and meals, and a wholesome understanding of silence in the presence of our elders was enforced with severity. Toys were forbidden us, even tennis rackets and bicycles were out of the question."[11] Though his father was a strict Victorian disciplinarian, Stacy-Judd recalled that he was "very distinguished looking," was partial to horse racing (owning his own horses), and loved to walk throughout London. "Father was a great walker and knew his London as no other man I have ever met . . . I was his constant companion on all his daily jaunts. It was then that we came closer to being real comrades than at any other time."[12]

STACY-JUDD WAS FIRST SENT TO ST. PAUL'S SCHOOL in Knightsbridge, London. When he was ten years old, his parents packed him off to a private boy's school at Campsil Glen, Scotland. He was there two to three years, and then returned to London where he was enrolled at Acton College. During his years at Acton College he lived at home "in a large house with many rooms. On the top floor one was allotted to me and I fitted it up as a workshop. Within the four walls of that room many weird and incongruous contraptions first saw the light of day. With a few, inadequate tools I made cameras and clocks, model sailing boats and steamships, telegraph instruments and electric devices and, in the year 1900, almost completed a working model aeroplane."[13] Included among these teenage inventions was also a small model submarine, which could operate under water.

Chapter 2

ON THE BASIS OF the numerous model ships which he designed and built, and particularly his design and construction of the model submarine, his father decided he should become a naval architect. Through friendship with one of the principals in the firm, his father arranged for his son to be articled for seven years to the famous naval architectural

firm of Yarrows. As an opening seemed some months in the future, his father temporarily abandoned articling his son to Yarrows. Instead he placed him temporarily with another, smaller London naval architectural firm, Mordant/Lawson & Co. Decorating the office walls of this concern led to his early dismissal.

AFTERWARDS, STACY-JUDD TRIED TO PERSUADE his father to let him pursue a career in architecture, but without success. After having attended a social event and thus incurring his father's anger, he decided it was time to leave home. He noticed an ad in the *London Daily Telegraph:*

Above, Model submarine, designed and constructed by Stacy-Judd, 1900.
Below, James Thompson residence, 1903, Southend-on-Sea, Sussex, England; (for James Thompson).

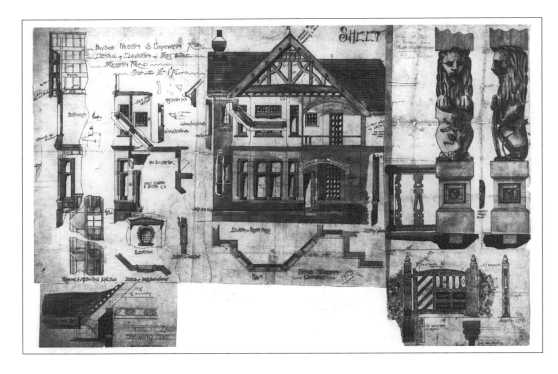

"An architect is prepared to receive a young gentleman as articled pupil."[14] The architect in question was James Thompson whose main office was located at West-Cliff-on-the-Sea, Sussex. Once again, Stacy-Judd's design for the model submarine opened the door, in this case into the world of architecture. "Hurriedly he [Thompson] glanced over them [Stacy-Judd's drawings] until he came to the last sample. This was the large sheet illustrating a submarine in plan, section, elevation and many details. At the same time, I thought he became interested in me."[15]

ALTHOUGH HE DID NOT HAVE THE 500 POUNDS needed for the articling, he was finally engaged by Thompson with a small sum for expenses. He remained in the Thompson office for four plus years, finishing his articles in 1904. While by no means a major figure on the European architectural scene, Thompson was a respected practitioner and designer. Like many other English "Edwardian" architects of the time, his design palette encompassed late versions of the Queen Anne, enriched by references to the Arts and Crafts vocabulary, and occasional exercises in the classical Beaux Arts revival, particularly in the then-fashionable revival of 18th-century English Georgian architecture.[16]

Metropole Hotel, Entrance Hall, 1903, Southend-on-Sea, Sussex, England; (for James Thompson).

Empire Hotel and Theatre, 1904-05, Birmingham, England; (for James Thompson).

THE MORE MEDIEVAL FLAVOR of Thompson's work can be seen in Stacy-Judd's 1903 drawings for the architect's own house. In contrast to the Tudor half-timbering and Arts and Crafts detailing of this house, Stacy-Judd's colored perspective drawings for the entrance hall for the Metropole Hotel, Southend-on-Sea (1903) and the seven-story Empire hotel in Birmingham present classical Beaux Arts schemes, both opulent with a vengeance. Since these latter schemes were apparently designed by Stacy-Judd, they serve as early examples of his own design abilities at the time.[17]

EVEN GRANTING THE ELABORATE BEAUX ARTS nature of his entrance hall design, it could only be described as outrageous. Certainly no one could ever consider it restrained, calm, or sophisticated. The quality of theatrical exaggeration and purposeful distortion which characterized his work throughout his life are both evident in this design.

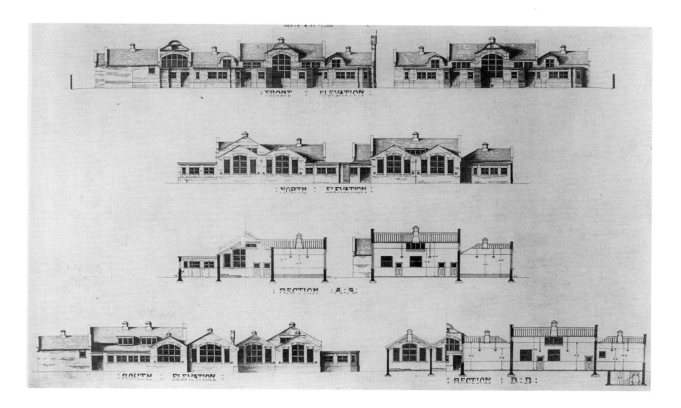

THE FEMALE DECORATIVE AND SCULPTURED FIGURES, nude and otherwise, are the central decorative motifs of his entrance hall design for the Metropole Hotel. These figures are outlandish in concept: one is precariously posed on one leg, holding aloft lanterns to light the newel-posts at the base of the stairs, while other female figures clutch onto the edge of an upper arch with one hand and balance an electric light in the other. The hall fireplace, with its oriel window, sports two richly framed round display windows. Female figures holding up the wide mantel shelf seem as impossible (that is, out of character) as the rest of the design.

IN STRIKING CONTRAST TO HIS BEAUX ARTS DESIGNS for both the Empire Hotel and the Metropole Hotel are the set of presentation drawings for a group of government schools on Bournmouth Park Road, Southend-on-Sea (1904). These schools partake of proto-modern designs associated with the English and Scottish Arts and Crafts movement, especially the work of Charles F. A. Voysey.[18] Their plans are ingenious, consisting of four modular blocks. The classrooms are arranged around a central assembly hall. Each classroom has its own

Above: Schools, Bournemouth Park 1904, Southend-on-Sea, Sussex, England; (for James Thompson; project).

gable roof and is lighted by large studio windows. The central assembly space, a story-and-a-half high, is lighted by wide flat-roofed dormer windows. The elevations closely reflect the varied interior spaces, and the surfaces of these elevations are quiet and highly abstract.

DURING THE THIRD YEAR (1903) of his articles he obtained summer leave so that he could further his architectural education by attending the South Kensington Science and Art Institute in London. He continued these classes, graduating in 1905, after he had left Thompson's office. After completing his articles, his first years in London were at best precarious. Often he did not have enough money for food, let alone to obtain any sort of housing. He visited numerous architectural offices, but to no avail. Finally he found a job as an minor assistant in a commercial laundry, followed by brief employment as a designer in a publicity firm. "As usual," he wrote, "the position was high, but the pay was low, very low. Sixteen shillings per week . . ."[19] This was followed by his job as a bartender in the seedy London district of St. Lukes.

WITH HIS EXPERIENCE IN ADVERTISING, he began to free-lance in this field. In the late summer and fall of 1905, he produced an illustrated brochure, "Humours of the History of Personal Adornment," for the

Kings Cross Hotel for the Great Northern Railroad Company, 1907-08, Kings Cross, London, England; (project).

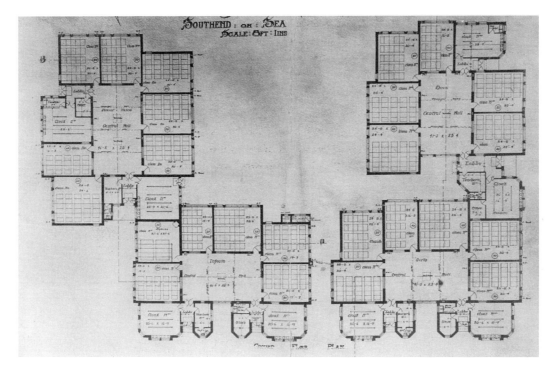

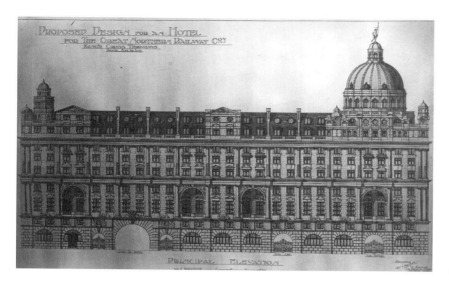

Left: Kings Cross Hotel for the Great
Northern Railroad Company, 1907-08,
Kings Cross, London; (project).
Below: Unidentified Office Building,
1906-07, West End, London,
England; (project).

Hatter and Hosier firm of T. J. Johnson of Southend-on-Sea. With humor, he played off the history of adornment, from Egyptian times to the present, suggesting with tongue-in-cheek that the Johnson firm had been around since 950 B.C. The drawings themselves are cartoonish, not to be taken any more seriously than the text.

A SIMILAR APPROACH WAS TAKEN for his second advertising brochure, "House Furnishing in the Stone Age," for William Jelks and Son in London. The illustrations accompanied by text were published as a series in the local newspapers, and then as a brochure to be handed out by the firm. Among his other advertising copy was a small booklet for H. P. Stroud and Son, a hairdressing firm in Tunbridge Wells. Like his other brochures, the one for Stroud consisted of text and drawings. The reader is introduced by the comment, "we dress the hairs of ladies and gentlemen with wondrous twists . . . of subtle wrists, in . . . ornamental hair we specialize; claim expertise in chiropody and dwell in an atmosphere of perfumery."[20]

BEFORE THESE INCURSIONS INTO THE WORLD of advertising, Stacy-Judd had applied for the position of architect to the Great Northern Railroad Company. In 1906, at the age of 22, he was appointed as architect and held this position through 1907. "My experience as a railway company architect progressed rapidly. There were always new buildings to be erected and considerable alterations and additions necessary to the firm's thousands of structures scattered throughout the country. I completed extensive surveys, valuations and

a variety of odd undertakings. I erected one hundred houses in Manchester, a similar number in Ruislip and scores of buildings elsewhere."[21]

THE HIGH POINT IN HIS WORK for the Great Northern Railroad Company was his design for a thousand-room hotel for their London Terminus at Kings Cross (1907-08). Though never built, his classically inspired design for the hotel represents one of the most correct and least perverse schemes of his career. The corner of the hotel is emphasized by a drum and dome, while the walls are divided horizontally into three-layered pilastered bands. At the ground level he provided arched entrance for cabs, and he provided openings within the rusticated basement for the public street railroad. Above the basement story he placed wide and deeply penetrating arches (similar to his design for the Empire Hotel) which break up the otherwise flat surface of the building.

WHILE WORKING FOR THE RAILROAD, Stacy-Judd attended drawing and design classes at the Regents Street Polytechnic School (1906-07) and also kept his eyes open for another position, for he realized that the job he held with the railroad was a dead end and would not lead to advancement. His attention was drawn to the announcement of the proposed Franco-British Exposition to be held in Shepherd's Bush, London. He applied for a position in the exposition's architectural office and was hired. He soon became the architect in charge of the Grounds Office for the exposition. Although he does mention doing some drawings and design for the exhibition, his name is not officially associated as an architect with any of the exposition buildings.[22]

AFTER COMPLETING HIS WORK at the exposition, he responded to an ad for an architect to join an established British firm in Buenos Aires, Argentina. Although he did not get the job, the idea of practicing architecture somewhere in the

Poster: "The Golden Gates of England," for City of Eastbourne, 1910.

Americas became a firm goal in his mind. For a brief time he worked as a government architect in the small community of Tunbridge Wells in Kent, but life as a governmental architect bored him. After recovering from an injury, he took an assumed name (Mr. Curtis) and developed "a profitable business designing decorative and humorous illustrations for publicity purposes."[23] While at Tunbridge Wells he had answered another ad, in this case for an editorship of a social journal, the *Eastbourne and Sussex Society Journal*. To his surprise he was offered the position, and became its editor for little over a year.

Egyptian Tablet recently unearthed, probable date, 950 B.C.

Illustration by Robert B. Stacy-Judd for his publication "Humours of the History of Personal Adornment," 1905.

WHILE WORKING FOR THIS PUBLICATION during 1909, he continued to carry on his advertising activities and later in the year, he started his own architectural practice. One of his publication projects at the time was the *Short-Story Time Table*.[24] The Time Tables were put out monthly, and they contained, in addition to the train timetables and other points of factual information, jokes, poems, notes and short stories by Stacy-Judd.

SEVERAL OF HIS LARGER DESIGN PROJECTS were displays for retail show windows. It is evident that they were as outlandish and exuberant as his architectural designs. "In one instance, I received a contract to take over the entire window space of a local furrier . . . We constructed a North Pole setting which included a large scale ship's prow breaking into the scene, and an explorer's encampment . . . the 'piece de resistance,' however, was provided by a man we sewed up in a bear skin. He looked and acted so realistically that, when the drapes were first drawn, an immense crowd blocked the sidewalk and two-thirds of the busy thoroughfare."[25]

THROUGHOUT 1909 AND 1910, Stacy-Judd continued his career in advertising. For the Christmas season at the Eastbourne stationer, R. Prentice, he took over the entire basement and constructed a series of mysterious caves, a model railroad and village, wishing wells, fortune tellers, hide-outs for children, and side shows. Visitors to Prentice's Christmas world were greeted by "Colia, Prince of the Forty Thieves, [who] stands at the door, in native costume", and

"The witch's Cave is inhabited by a real witch with steaming cauldron over fire."[26] The North Pole and these displays indicate his interest in non-European exotica.

A FURTHER INSTANCE OF THIS INTEREST is evident in one of a series of posters he designed to advertise the city of Eastbourne. Why Eastbourne should be thought of as "The Golden Gates of England," is one matter, but even more bizarre is the Islamic setting of this poster, including two figures, one of whom is kneeling and greeting the sun as it arises over Eastbourne. As with most of his drawings, the poster employed brilliant and highly contrasting colors. Since one assumes that the task of the poster was to attract attention quickly with its garish colors and flamboyant and puzzling subject matter, it certainly must have succeeded.

As A RESULT OF HIS CHRISTMAS DESIGN, Stacy-Judd was engaged to design a four-story building for the Prentice firm in Eastbourne. "The Prentice contract was the first real architectural commission I ever secured. It was the first opportunity I had to hang out my shingle with a full sense of its significance."[27]

ALTHOUGH HE DID NOT ABANDON his enterprising life in advertising or his editorship of the *Short-Story Timetable* and the *Eastbourne and Sussex Society Journal,* he at long last established his own architectural office.

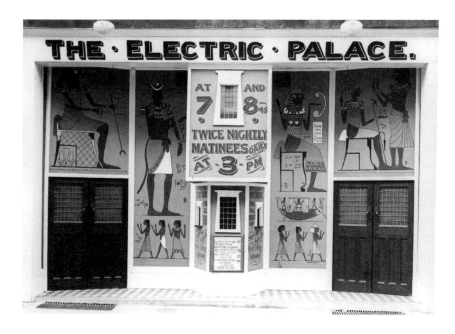

Electric Picture Palace, 1910-12, Ventor, Isle of Wight, England.

Interior, Electric Picture Palace, 1910-12, Ventnor, Isle of Wight, England.

STACY-JUDD'S NEXT CLIENT, ERNEST MANSELL, set the stage for a new quirk in his career. For this client he remodeled a second floor hall into a motion picture theater (1909-1910). In this project he plunged once again into an exotic world, the Egyptian. "I designed and painted a mural which completely filled the large area surrounding the proscenium opening. The subject was a descriptive story told in heroic-size Egyptian figures."[28] The Mansell Theater at Eastbourne was followed by two other theaters for the same client: one in London, Mansell's Marylebone Electric Palace (1910), and the other the Electric Picture Palace (1910-12) in the town of Ventnor on the Isle of Wight. In addition to designing these theaters, Stacy-Judd also invested his savings in them.

WRITING OF THIS EXPERIENCE HE NOTED that while "I enjoyed the unusual experience during my association with the Marylebone theater and, incidentally appreciated the profits there from, I looked upon the venture as a means to an end. Always I bore in mind my decision to leave England at the earliest possible moment."[29] The business that prevented him from leaving was his design and financial involvement with the construction of the Ventnor theater.

FOR THE DESIGN OF THE ELECTRIC PALACE, he expanded on the Egyptian theme, both for the exterior and for the interior. The street facade presented an abbreviated Egyptian pylon; within the opening of the pylon were situated the ticket booth and the entrances to the theater. The exterior walls were divided into panels and within them Egyptian figures [painted by Stacy-Judd] in bright colors dominated the scenes.

DURING CONSTRUCTION MANSELL OVEREXTENDED himself and went into bankruptcy, and Stacy-Judd, to protect his financial investments in the project, had to assume ownership of the theater. His description of how he dealt with his creditors, completed the construction of the theater, and arranged in his usual flamboyant fashion a highly successful advertising campaign to make the theater known illustrates his abilities to sell a product, whether in this case the film program of a motion picture theater, or later in the twenties, the "All-American" Maya style of architecture.

WHILE IN VENTNOR, Stacy-Judd prepared drawings for an "Escalator," (1911) to go from the upper cliff's edge to the beach. The little building which he provided at the lower entrance to the funicular is akin to a medieval lich gate. Like many of his designs, this one draws attention because it is odd. The asymmetry of the scheme with its low sloping roof that comes close to the ground and the open knee-brace which meets this roof is not at all what one would expect.

Escalator, 1911, Battery, Ventor, Isle of Wight, England; (project).

ANOTHER PROJECT AT THE END OF 1912 was a second new theater for Ventnor, the Palace Theatre. Although this theater was planned with a stage house, it was primarily to be used for motion pictures. His design for the street facade of the theater was "Old English"; that is, English Tudor. The lower level was sheathed in brick with stone trim, while the upper section, including the central gable, was half-timbered. A wide stucco band was left free within the half-timbering so that the lighted name of the theater could be of an appropriately large scale. Just above the projecting glass and metal marquee were groups of three windows which helped to light the entrance lobby. The overall proportions of the Palace

Theater are, as is usual in his designs, peculiar; the upper half-timbered gable area is proportionately much too large in its relationship to the lower level, which seems to be squashed under the weight of the half-timbered gable.

BEFORE HE SOLD THE ELECTRIC PALACE THEATER and was finally off to America, he experienced in 1911 the drama of his first air flight. The town of Ventnor organized an airplane meet, and Stacy-Judd became a member of the sponsoring committee. "The second day of the aviation meet, Gordon England invited me to go up with him. I jumped at the opportunity."[30] England's airplane developed mechanical problems, so Stacy-Judd went up instead with Henry Roland Fleming. Fleming and his passenger were barely able to get off the ground and just missed falling into the ocean. "Slowly, ever so slowly we continued to rise. How those sticks of bamboo, wire and linen held together, I'll never know. But, in spite of my concern for its ability, in spite of the din, the shaking and rush of wind, it was a thrilling ride."[31]

Palace Theatre, 1912, Ventnor, Isle of Wight, England; (project).

Emery Mapes residence, 1914, Minneapolis, Minnesota; (project).

Off to the Americas

IN 1911 STACY-JUDD DECIDED TO VISIT CANADA first and then the United States, followed by working his way down to Buenos Aires where he hoped to establish himself professionally. "Buenos Aires originally was the objective but my talks with fellow travelers [on the boat] somewhat lessened my determination. So I resolved to permit fate to do with me as she wished."[32] His ship arrived in Quebec. Thence he traveled across the whole of Canada to Vancouver in British Columbia.

He was tempted to stay and establish himself in Victoria, but decided to first experience the United States before making a decision.

FROM SEATTLE HE TOOK THE GREAT NORTHERN TRAIN across the U.S., stopping along the way at the principal cities. Of the Midwestern cities, the community that interested him most was Minneapolis. In the Northeast he observed, "Boston is Boston, staunch in politics, tea parties, customs and a pardonable pride of ancestry."[33] New York did not sit well with him. He described it as "The city of monuments to the ego of man. The city of artificial canyons of steel and stone, feebly defiant of natural law, yet frantically persistent. A metropolis dedicated to function but without form; a futile experiment in massed structure and massed humanity. Soul-less."[34]

HIS TRAVELS IN THE U.S. DISSUADED HIM FROM the idea of going to South America. Instead the lure of the vast open spaces of the Midwest enticed him to establish his architectural practice in Minneapolis, where he had already made a few acquaintances. He had barely rented space and set up his office when he met a hardware salesman who knew of an architect in Minot, North Dakota, who was looking for a partner. Stacy-Judd wrote to him, received a favorable response, and then took the train, arriving at Minot in April, 1914. He noted of his first impression of the place that it "left me without the slightest enthusiasm. From a professional standpoint, I saw nothing to warrant a future . . . . Of architecture, there was no sign. It was not a matter of the profession being at a low ebb; it was simply unborn."[35]

COMPARED TO HIS EXPERIENCES IN ENGLAND, and even in the major cities he had visited in Canada and the United States, North Dakota was indeed devoid of many professional architects. But his blanket judgment that "Of architecture, there was no sign," was somewhat overdrawn.[36] There was a scattering of well-designed late nineteenth, early twentieth-century buildings within North Dakota, especially in such communities as Bismarck, Grand Forks, Jamestown and Wahpeton. There was even a sprinkling of the then-fashionable Craftsman dwellings, accompanied by a scattering of avant-garde Prairie-style buildings by Purcell and Elmslie and others. In a PR release published in the December 1917 issue of *The Western Architect,*

Chapter 3

"The Trials of the Pioneer Architect," Stacy-Judd, as is usual, somewhat overstates his contribution to North Dakota architecture.[37] His portrait of himself as a pioneer akin to the earlier settlers of the East and Midwest is overdrawn, but still, it must be admitted there were not many architects who lived and practiced in the Dakotas during the first two decades of this century.[38]

Elks Home, 1914-15, Williston, ND (with R.T. Frost).

ACCORDING TO STACY-JUDD, the Minot architect R. T. Frost painted a glowing picture of the prospects for an architect in the Dakotas, especially in Minot. With much misgiving, Stacy-Judd was finally persuaded to try the place at least for a short time and formed a partnership with him.[39] His intention of staying only briefly had to be thrown aside when he awoke "one morning with the knowledge that my entire capital had vanished . . . For good and sufficient reasons, I had been induced to invest practically every dollar I possessed."[40] What this project he invested in was not mentioned in his autobiography. Whatever his reasons, he remained in North Dakota until 1918, when he became involved in wartime housing in the East.

HIS FIRST COMMISSION UNDERTAKEN within his brief partnership with Frost was the Elks Home in Williston, North Dakota (1914-15).[41] Williston, whose population at the time was around 6,500, was located some 120 miles west of Minot via the Great Northern Railroad (both of these communities Stacy-Judd had traveled through during his earlier trip across the country). For the image of the Elks Home, he turned to the half-timber Tudor Revival, then very popular in both England and the United States. As with most of his designs, there is a seemingly cultivated awkwardness about the building, in its proportions, and in the scale of windows and doors. He sheathed the lower floor with shingles, which because of their dark color, suggest brick, and then, he went full force on the second floor and in the gable ends with an overly rich pattern of half-timbering. The project was built much as designed, except his central fountain centering on a standing nude female figure was not carried out.

EITHER DESIGNED IN MINNEAPOLIS, or just after he joined Frost, was the projected Emory Mapes house (1914) in Minneapolis. This too is Tudoresque, but in this instance the design conveys a child-like lack of reality. It appears more as a drawing for a late nineteenth-century fairy tale than a building which might be constructed. The half-timbering is carried out with a vengeance, not one section of the exterior surface remains plain and undecorated. Even wilder than usual was the surrounding garden with its array of garden sculpture, terraces, stairs, and meandering paths. The whole landscape design has the delightful ambience of a miniature golf course with its dollhouse-like buildings and lilliputian landscape.

WITHIN A FEW MONTHS OF ARRIVING in Minot, he severed his partnership with Frost and set up his own practice. As in the past, he became an aggressive entrepreneur for his wares. He describes how he selected a town north of Minot and traveled there to see about possible commissions. The town in question was Crosby, a county seat in the northwest corner of the state. "The town I selected stood on a snow-clad prairie and looked for all the world like a piece of toast on a barren table cloth. There was one main street running north and south on which stood one hotel, two banks, the one general store and a few off places of business."[42] He then proceeded to play off the town's two bankers, telling each of them that the other was planning on building a new facility. The president of the First State Bank fell for the bait and commissioned Stacy-Judd to design a new building for him.

Stacy-Judd's North Dakota designs of the mid-teens illustrate the usual wide variety of images found in the work of most American architectural practitioners of those years. For domestic designs he preferred the popular English Tudor. For institutional and commercial buildings he wavered back and forth between something which perhaps could be described as a stripped rationalism, to the use of the vertical Gothic for multi-story buildings, at times almost Prairie-esque, to a full-fledged acceptance of the classical Beaux Arts tradition. For his own house of 1916-19, in Minot, he certainly absorbed the atmosphere of the late Craftsman movement. The form of this two-story house, with its wide overhanging gable roof, horizontal banks of windows and half-timbering evokes the image of a Swiss Chalet. The plan of his own house is unusual in that the main living space is on the second level. At this level one enters a glass porch and beyond the living room, lighted by a wide glass bay along one wall and terminating at the other side in a half-timbered inglenook with an odd corner fireplace. Below on the ground level, a sheltered loggia looked out to the south, and behind the grand over scaled entrance stairs, was a garage which was integral to the house.

One of the many cultivated mysteries surrounding his life, was his marriage to Anna Veronica in Minneapolis in 1917. (We are not

Above: Blakey Block, 1916, Minot, ND.
Below: Exterior illustration of Robert B.
Stacy-Judd Residence, 1916-19,
Minot, ND.

certain whether Veronica was his wife's last name or not; Stacy-Judd does not mention her at all in his autobiography. They were divorced in Los Angeles in 1922).

Interior, Robert B. Stacy-Judd Residence, 1916-19, Minot, Minnesota ND.

NATIONAL GUARD ARMORIES, from the nineteenth century on, had been cast in the form of a medieval castle. Stacy-Judd followed suit with his 1915 Armory at Williston, North Dakota. At the corner of the building was a large rounded tower, appropriately crenelated. A medieval keep-like form rises from the rear of the building, and small make-believe turrets guard the various entrances. To reinforce his castle image he introduced crenelation on other sections of the buildings. For the angled entrance tower to the Bethania Lutheran Church (1915) at Minot, he employed crenelation, and an abstracted reference to crenelation occurs in his otherwise mildly Prairie-esque Public School (l917) at Des Lacs, North Dakota.

THE TWO-STORY GARAGE AND APARTMENT BLOCK for Ely and Young in Minot (1917) must have been responded to as modern at the time, expressed in its system of repeated bays derived from the Midwest Prairie mode and the stripped classicism which was eventually to develop into the Art Deco of the mid to late twenties. Out and out

classical Beaux Arts designs were two large scale projects which were never carried out. These were the six-story Second National Bank and Office Building (1915), and the richly ornamented Farmers Rural Credit Association building (1919), both in Minot.

SOMEWHERE IN BETWEEN THE RATIONAL and the Beaux Arts classical imagery was his eight-story Hotel Minot (1914), a commission he designed after he left his partnership with Frost. The street level of the hotel was to have been of highly rusticated masonry, while the surfaces above were to have been dealt with in a very flat fashion. The ends of the upper floors and the second level were to be tied together to suggest two towers each to be surmounted by horizontal bases and low drums.

THE WILDEST OF STACY-JUDD'S Midwestern designs was his temporary stage-set for the Northwestern North Dakota Auto Show of 1916, in Minot. The derivation of the design is obvious, as a photograph shows that Stacy-Judd's office in Minot had his colorful Islamic-inspired Eastbourne poster prominently displayed above his reading table. For his Auto Show stage set, he took this exotic Islamic theme, multiplied the cusped arches and added domes to create the illusion of a Moorish courtyard, occupied not by fountains and flowers as in his poster, but by the latest models of automobiles. His design was a play of three-dimensional elements with a twenty-five by fifty-foot mural (painted, of course, by Stacy-Judd).

Above: Public School, 1917, Des Lacs, ND.

IN HIS AUTOBIOGRAPHY STACY-JUDD claimed that his two-and-a-half-story La Due Apartment building (1916) in Williston, North Dakota was the "first all-pressed steel frame structure in the U.S."[43] As with most of his assertions of being first, it is difficult to know whether his claim is really valid. Photographs of the building under construction clearly reveal its thin metal frame, though no evidence of this frame remained visible once the building was sheathed in multicolor brick. But whether first or not, this use of thin pressed steel members for a small apartment building was quite unusual for those years. Hollow terra cotta tile and reinforced concrete were occasionally used for buildings of this size in the teens and twenties, but seldom did small domestic buildings utilize a frame of pressed steel. His use of this "modern" material indicates how quickly he absorbed what was new on the American scene.

THE TASK OF ESTABLISHING HIS ARCHITECTURAL PRACTICE in North Dakota led to a variety of entanglements. First was the problem

of obtaining reasonable fees for his services. At that time the national
American Institute of Architects had set a six percent figure as the low-
est to be accepted. But in the Dakotas, the usual was one to one-and-
a-half percent; a level of remuneration almost impossible to live on.

Stacy-Judd fought hard for the higher figure and
won. He also found himself involved in a long battle (in the courts and out) with the state contractors association. According to Stacy-Judd, the
members of the association wished him to avoid
open bidding by their parceling out the job to one
of their members. For this favor, they would pay a
small "kick-back" to the architect. Stacy-Judd said
no, and after many difficulties lasting over several
years, he, along with several other architects, was
able to break up the solidity of the contractors'
association. His activities upon the behalf of his
profession led to his appointment in 1917, to the
North Dakota Board of Architectural Examiners,
though it would appear that he was not able to
serve because he was not an American citizen.

WHILE PRACTICING IN NORTH DAKOTA, Stacy-Judd kept up his literary efforts. He produced more poetry, as well as articles for the local Minot newspaper. He wrote and illustrated a piece on the "'Mint House' Pevensey, Sussex, England," for the Minneapolis publication, *The Western Architect*.[44] He gathered together a number of local stories and published these as *Tales from Old Times*. He also wrote a "problem play" *Dracula,* which was performed in Minot, and described in the local newspaper as "a gripping, human interest story."[45]

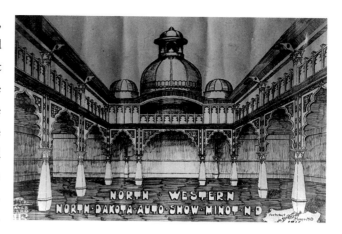

Above: Northwestern North Dakota Automobile Show, 1915, Minot, ND.
Below: La Due Apartment Building, 1915-16, Williston, ND.

WHEN THE UNITED STATES ENTERED the First World War in 1918, Stacy-Judd "journeyed to Washington and offered myself for public service, passed the necessary physical examination, and then waited. As it happened, I was chosen not for the fighting service but as one of the eight supervisors in charge of all construction work undertaken by the Housing Division of the United States Emergency Fleet Corporation. Three projects were allocated to me, to be constructed simultaneously. One at Lorain, Ohio; one at Wyandotte, Michigan and the third at Manitowoc, Wisconsin. From the central office in Philadelphia, I supervised the construction of hundreds of homes and other buildings."[46]

FUNDS FOR THE EMERGENCY SHIP Workers Housing Act were granted by Congress in March 1, 1918. This funding together with a presidential Executive Order authorized the Emergency Fleet Corporation to produce new housing and local transportation systems.[47] The nationally-known planner and landscape architect Frederick Law Olmsted, Jr. was appointed the manager of the Town Planning Division of the Corporation.[48]

THE THREE PRINCIPAL PROJECTS which Stacy-Judd worked on were modest additions to existing cities. His responsibility was twofold: to supervise the physical layout of these new developments (roads, utilities, etc.) and then, to see that the single family and multiple housing units were built. All of this was to be accomplished as rapidly as possible. In these projects, he certainly applied directly the lessons he had learned from his earlier supervision of the construction of the 1907-8 Franco-British Exposition in London. As with his earlier experience, there is no indication that he was involved in the design of either of the sites or the housing; although as the on-site supervising architect, he probably made some design changes as these projects proceeded.

La Due Apartment Building, 1915-16, Williston, ND.

The Canadian Interlude

WHEN THE WAR ENDED, Stacy-Judd returned briefly to Minot in 1919, but it seemed by then he had decided to move to central Canada. He had probably entered, in 1919, into a discussion of a partnership with the Canadian architect William B. Major.[49] After another legal battle in a long stream, he left the Dakotas for a new chapter in his professional career, this time in the province of Alberta. Stacy-Judd established himself in Calgary, which at the time had a population of some 90,000 people. The central portion of Alberta had been enjoying a tremendous boom in population, agriculture, and manufacturing from 1910 well on into the early twenties. "During the first year alone," wrote Stacy-Judd, "we completed over one million dollars worth of contracts without the aid of a single assistant. Considering the type and class of structures [they] were not pretentious, this meant our noses were on the grindstone almost continually."[50]

THE MAJOR PROJECT REALIZED in his two-and-a-half year partnership with Major was the Empire Theater and Apartment building in Edmonton (1920).[51] The imagery of the building varied appreciably from one vantage point to another. The exterior with its slighted pointed arches hinted at the Tudor-esque medieval. In contrast, the entrance lobby with its tiled walls and wrought iron lights conveys a late Arts and Crafts atmosphere. The auditorium itself is not easy to pin down stylistically, but it is essentially Adamesque with touches of Georgian baroque. Stacy-Judd noted of this project that he "designed all of the interior decorations, furnishings, electrical fixtures and plaster ornaments."[52] As one would expect, he produced the design for the draped, picture framed rococo fire screen for the stage as well as the five curved ceiling paintings of the proscenium arch. The subject of the screen is a classical garden centering on a pair of nude female sculptures in front of a pergola garden structure. The paintings contained in the proscenium arch present a variety of classical allegories resplendent with putti and other gallant figures. As with all of his formal drawings and painting these have a cartoonish atmosphere, which suggests both playfulness and incompleteness.

WITH THE COMPLETION OF THIS THEATER and with his earlier background in designing theaters in England, Stacy-Judd and his partner Major received several other commissions for theaters for both legitimate stage productions and the increasingly popular motion pictures. For their smaller buildings such as houses, Major and Stacy-Judd often turned to the English Tudor. Except for Stacy-Judd's weird garden scene in this case centering on a circular pool with a small bridge and central sun dial, their Edmund Taylor house (1919) in Calgary is similar to other Tudor image houses found throughout Canada. Employing a similar image, with touches of the primitive frontier, was their ranch house for the Earl of Minto (1920), situated near Nanton.

Chapter 4

ONE OF THE MOST INTERESTING of their smaller buildings was a service station for the Imperial Oil Company situated in Calgary (1921). The design is characteristic for the time, with a pair of stone piers supporting a projecting gable roof over the pump area. The gabled ends are half-timbered, and a wainscot of clinker brick sheathes the lower section of the walls. Cast and wrought iron columns topped by lanterns conceal the fact that they are pumps, and the building is set in one of Stacy-Judd's formal gardens with a circular flower bed centering on a small fountain, pool and the essential female sculptured figure.

EVEN THOUGH HIS DAYS were taken up with his practice, Stacy-Judd still found time to write. He produced a series of articles on architecture during the winter and early spring months of 1922 which were published in the *Calgary Daily Herald*.[53] These were entitled "Chats on Practical Architecture," and they were either signed by Stacy-Judd or labeled as authored by "Buildicus." The articles were meant to introduce the middle-class reader (potential clients, of course) to the subject of architecture, the need to employ architects, and then such subjects as

Empire Theatre and Apartment Block, 1920, Edmonton, Alberta, Canada; (with W.P. Major).

asbestos shingles, incinerators, the advantage of the bungalow as a house type, and discussions of various types of business and office blocks.

ALTHOUGH IT MAY NOT have been his prime intent, Stacy-Judd still presented a clear picture of his views of architecture in these articles. In the fourth article he wrote of the "laws of architecture" and notes that "In modern times that same sense of symmetry, pose and adaption are needed in the design of the modern skyscraper, the

public building and the modern home . . . . Without the knowledge of the history of architecture no man is qualified to practice. The knowledge gleaned from six thousand years B.C. to present times, with its tribal laws, its classical principles, its medieval conditions, is the basis upon which modern building wonders are founded. The knowledge gathered from the ancient fountains of art grant us the language whereby we compose poems and prose according to our inventive ability."[54]

LIKE MANY OTHER ARCHITECTS IN THE WEST, whether in Canada or the United States, Stacy-Judd responded warmly to the bungalow as the ideal middle-class house type. "In modern times a type of dwelling has evolved which easily takes first place as the ideal home. I

Above: Interior of the Empire Theatre, 1920, Edmonton, Alberta, Canada. Below: L. R. Earl of Minto Ranch House, 1920, Nanton, Alberta Canada; (with W.P. Major).

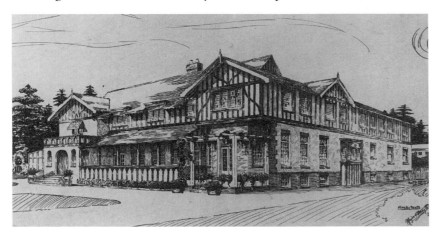

refer to the bungalow. The term originated, no doubt in India, but the bungalow of that country is not in comparison with its modern namesake. The most popular type is what is known as the 'California'."[55] In the planning of the "modern house" (including, of course, the bungalow) he argued for informality, for combining living and dining spaces into one room, for providing sunny [ideally facing towards the east] breakfast nooks off the kitchen, and for laying out the basement so that it could provide space for a family gaming room. His observations about eliminating interior details which "are breeding grounds for unwelcome germs and a remarkably effective resting place for dust," is similar to the puritanical arguments of the early California modernist, Irving J. Gill.[56]

THESE ARTICLES FOR THE CALGARY NEWSPAPER also revealed his enthusiasm for the latest technical gadgets and techniques of construction. He assumed that commercial buildings would be built of either reinforced concrete or steel frame,[57] and for the single family he "recommended as a first-class method of house construction . . . a pressed steel frame." Mirroring the approach taken by most architects of these years, Stacy-Judd embraced all of the latest in building technology, but technology had little to do with the aesthetic aspects of his architecture. Imagery was one thing, technology another.

On to California

"DURING THE WINTER OF 1921-22, I saw the handwriting on the wall," noted Stacy-Judd. "Business was rapidly going on a downward trail, and it looked like a long one. So in the spring of 1922, I drove down to California to sum up conditions and prospects. A week's investigation induced me to return to Canada, pack up my belongings and migrate to Los Angeles."[58] Every trip of his seemed to turn out to be a series of adventures, and in this instance, an adventure like a Hollywood Wild West film. He eluded bandits after a long breathtaking chase on the highway south of Portland, Oregon, and just barely escaped from a raging forest fire.

IN HIS AUTOBIOGRAPHY STACY-JUDD MENTIONS that he established his practice in Hollywood in the late fall of 1922. It is possible though that he may have arrived in the Southland somewhat earlier than this, for the Santa Barbara architect Lutah Maria Riggs mentioned that an English architect by the name of "Stacy" came to work for a few months in the Montecito office of George Washington Smith on August 22, 1922.[59] Whether this was Stacy-Judd remains an intriguing question.

ONE ASSUMES THAT STACY-JUDD already knew a few people in the Southland, for within a few months after he had established his office he was able to hire several draftspersons and had a number of commissions in hand. His work in Los Angeles in the first few years encompassed a diverse set of Period Revival architectural images, ranging from the English and French medieval to Mediterranean and Spanish, the Egyptian and the Islamic, to variations on the theme of the woodsy California bungalow.

THE BEN HANSEN HOUSE (1923) IN BRENTWOOD HEIGHTS was essentially a low lying California bungalow, sheathed in redwood board and batten (stained a light green), but characteristic of his designs, it had several jarring notes. The entrance doorway is reminiscent of a circular Chinese moon gate, "the first of this type Mr. Stacy-Judd designed in California."[60] The second unusual feature of this house is the high flat-roofed section of the building, which, in strong contrast to the low pitched gable roofed section, is treated as a tall rectangular volume surmounted by a broadly extended flat roof. Directly below the wide overhanging roof is a wide stucco band containing stenciled patterns which seem to have been derived from both Vienna c. 1900 and from Native American designs. Other similar stenciled motifs were carried out on the corner pilasters and on the sides of the principal stucco chimney.

PROBABLY RESPONDING TO CLIENT'S WISHES, he continued to produce Craftsman/Tudor houses; a case in point is the hillside Bishop house (1923) in Sparr Heights, Los Angeles. As he was prone to do, he countered the informality of the house with one of his strange formal gardens: an entrance garden domi-

Chapter 5

nated by a long oval flower bed, formally defined by a low hedge, and a smaller self-contained garden by the entrance steps that exhibited his usual pool containing a dancing nude female figure.

AS ONE WOULD EXPECT OF AN ARCHITECT practicing in Southern California in the twenties, he quickly took over the popular Hispanic/Mediterranean imagery. Examples of this mode are his store

Above: Jensen's Theatre, 1923,
Los Angeles.
Below: Bishop House, 1923, Glendale.

32

building for Leona's Importation (1923) in Los Angeles, in a Proposed Hotel (1924) at Beaumont, and in a Projected Bungalow Court (1923) in Sparr Heights, Los Angeles.

STACY-JUDD'S FASCINATION WITH THE EXOTIC in architecture found a warm and appreciative audience in Los Angeles during the 1920s. For the projected Beni-Hasan Theater and accompanying stores and offices (1923) in Arcadia, he looked, as he had several times in the past, to the architecture of ancient Egypt. The interior of the theater boasts overscaled sculptured figures of the pharaohs, and for the painted stage curtain he produced the front of the Temple of Hathor at Dendera, probably taken from a plate in Banister Fletcher's often

Above: Ben Hansen House, 1923, Brentwood Heights.
Below: Exterior illustration of Ben Hansen House, 1923, Brentwood Heights.

consulted *A History of Architecture on the Comparative Method*.[61] As with so many of his projects, the building was planned in a functionally inventive manner with the theater set behind a row of two-story stores and offices. One entered the theater's entrance court through a low pylon. The theater auditorium and stage house, at right angles to the entrance, were treated as an even larger pylon. If it had been built, the Beni-Hasan Theater would in its extravagance have out-Egypted the somewhat later well-known Egyptian Theater in Hollywood.[62]

Above: House in Beverly Ridge, 1927; (project).

34

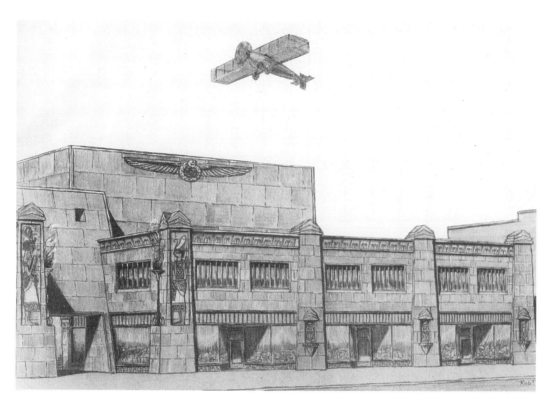

Above and below: The Beni-Hasan Theatre, Store and Office Building, 1923-24, Arcadia; (project).

Aztec Hotel, Monrovia, 1924-25 (detail).

The Aztec Hotel

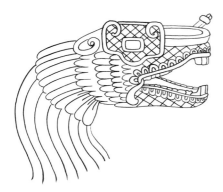

WITHIN A YEAR OR SO OF HIS ARRIVAL in Southern California two incidents occurred which opened up for him a new world of architectural imagery and ideology. In the summer of 1923, he was commissioned to design a group of West Coast hotels for National Community Hotels, Inc. (Hockenbury Systems, Inc.) of Harrisburg, Pennsylvania. A few months later, he was introduced to the pre-Columbian architecture of Mexico and Central America, especially of the Maya. The timing and coalescing of these two events, together with the atmosphere of exoticism of the Hollywood film, led to the most widely acclaimed building of his career, the Aztec Hotel (1924-25) in Monrovia.[63]

HOW AND WHEN STACY-JUDD came in contact with the managers of the Pennsylvania hotel chain is not revealed in his letters or autobiography. One would assume that he was not reticent in advertising the fact that he had already designed hotels (projected and built) in England and Canada. For example, his large scale, colorful and elaborate drawings for some of his hotels were on display on the walls of his Hollywood offices for perspective clients to see (and hopefully admire). Added to these examples he let people know about his experience as a successful businessman-showman in designing and operating motion picture theaters in England. A hotel, like a theater, must compete and sell its wares and services, and in Southern California the competition, as he pointed out, was fierce.

STACY-JUDD HAD ALREADY FONDLY EMBRACED the exotic architecture of the non-European scene, the world of ancient Egypt and of Islam, to promote his theaters, sell tourism, and to market automobiles. In writing about the Aztec Hotel in Monrovia he showed his enthusiasm for the exotic when he wrote "I am, and have been for many years, exceedingly interested in Egyptian architecture and the arts of the Orient . . . Indulgent clients allowed me to express my Egyptian interpretations in theaters and homes."[64]

IN SOUTHERN CALIFORNIA, the eye-catching examples of ancient Egypt and of Islamic architecture (as well as of Japan, China, and of ancient Assyria and Babylon), plus pure programatic buildings (buildings in the form of ice cream cones, toads, oranges, etc.) were images used to advertise everything from real estate to fast food establishments, hotels and theaters. Although Los Angeles and Southern California did not boast as many of these exotic architectural images as is usually thought, there still were enough around to be in evidence and, more importantly, they were noticed and presented by East Coast and European editors and authors as typical of the L.A. scene.

THUS, WISHING TO RECEIVE ATTENTION for their buildings, Stacy-Judd and the national and local management of the hotel chain needed a design which would command attention. In the teens and twenties

Chapter 6

Exterior of the Aztec Hotel, Monrovia, 1924-25.

a design needed a fairy tale quality about to catch attention. It needed to take individuals from the prosaic world of everyday life to some distant and romantic place, not only from the normal experience of the American middle and upper middle class, but far away in time, similar to the type of exoticism presented in the new silent motion pictures.

ALTHOUGH, AS MENTIONED, the details of circumstances which brought the hotel commissions into his office are unknown, the events which led to his (close to religious) conversion to the cause of the revival of pre-Columbian architecture of Mexico and Central America as a new inspirational source for him are known. "It all started," he wrote, "with a salesman of architectural books who paid me monthly visits . . . . One day in the fall of 1923, he made one of his usual calls. I told him I was too busy to look at books. Little did I dream of the importance of this interview. 'I have two specials here for you,' he urged. 'Sorry, I haven't the time to look at them.' 'Quite unusual. . .Nothing like them. If you haven't time now, keep 'em here, three months, six months, I don't care. If you don't want 'em then, that's O.K. too.' 'Gosh!' the bookseller said, 'they're some funny looking cuts in 'em. Printed some eighty years ago, what d'you know about that, and I don't know a thing about 'em. Never heard of the subject before. I thought you'd be the most likely man to want 'em' [the latter comment reveals that the book salesman sensed Stacy-Judd's taste for the way-out and exotic]."

Lobby of the Aztec Hotel.

"STILL PROTESTING, I IDLY SPUN THE PAGES. Illustrations appeared in profusion, strange illustrations showing the most extraordinary-looking buildings I had ever seen. Some were of plain, simple design, yet of dignified and classical proportions. Others bore elaborate and very original carvings. In all instances the buildings were shown surrounded and overgrown with dense jungle. I stared at each picture, fascinated. It was the most interesting, most entrancing subject imaginable. I turned to the title page and read *Incidents of Travel in Central America, Chiapas and Yucatan* by John L. Stephens, 1841. For some unaccountable reason, I suddenly knew I wanted these books more than anything on earth. I purchased them on the spot."[65]

THE TWO-VOLUME SET WHICH STACY-JUDD purchased had become a much sought after classic almost from the moment it was published. While the text by the nineteenth-century travel writer John L. Stephens is engaging and fascinating, what sold the books were the impressive set of woodcut plates. They were based upon the drawings of the architect/artist Frederick Catherwood[66] who was trained in England as an architect, and early developed an impressive ability for topographical rendering. In his drawings, he carried on the eighteenth-century tradition of a deep admiration for the romantic and picturesque.

A key to the understanding of the picturesque was entailed in the concept
of the sublime, most clearly found in the writings of the eighteenth-
century Irish literatus, Edmund Burke. The nature of the sublime was
beautifully realized in Catherwood's drawings. The funerary sense
of decay, of melancholy, of man and his creations being eventually
subsumed by nature are the central themes of his drawings which
illustrated the Stephen's volumes.

"A MONTH OR SO PRIOR TO THE BOOK INCIDENT," wrote
Stacy-Judd, "I had been appointed by the Hockenbury System of
Harrisburg, Pennsylvania, architect for western America. For the firm
I designed many hotels, but the first project to be considered, although
by no means the largest, became the most important work of my life.[67]
The floor plan for this structure had just been completed and I was
about to commence designing the elevations, or exteriors, for this
building when Stephen's books came into my hands . . . . Purely as an
experiment, I adapted motifs from the decorative details of the art
illustrated in Stephen's two volumes."[68]

THE FOLLOWING MORNING STACY-JUDD'S OFFICE staff were
exposed to the project. Their comment was "'Maya! Never heard of it,
but whatever it is, you've got something there.' The chief draftsman
added somewhat prophetically 'You get that design erected and it

The Lobby, looking west, the Aztec Hotel.

won't be the last you'll hear of it.' This encouraging remark coming from the chief draftsman, whose usual biting criticism I highly valued, surprised me, because, until that moment I had not the slightest intention of asking my clients to accept such an unconventional design for their hotel. I had merely felt an uncontrollable urge at the time to experiment with the strange motifs displayed in Stephen's book. However, I then and there decided to submit the design to the hotel board of directors . . ."[69]

STACY-JUDD THEN TURNED SHOWMAN with his clients, showing them first a design "in the Spanish style," and then letting them get a glimpse of his Maya fantasy. They quickly were "sold" on the unusual appeal of his Maya design, and they authorized him to proceed with it. As he mentioned, the plan for the Aztec Hotel was arrived at before he clothed it in Maya motifs. His sense of salesmanship was well illustrated in the name he chose for the hotel. He wrote that "when the hotel project was first announced, the word Maya was unknown to the layman. The subject of Maya culture was merely of archaeological importance, and, at that, concerned but a few exponents. As the word Aztec was fairly well known, I baptized the hotel with that name, although all the decorative motifs are Maya."[70]

THE SCHEME FOR THE AZTEC HOTEL was an L-shaped building enclosing a rear patio which enjoyed a northern view of the nearby San Gabriel mountains. The building included the usual array of spaces found in a small suburban hotel: a number of private rooms with baths, a spacious entrance and lobby, and a dining room which opened onto a portal adjoining a patio and informal garden. In addition, there were eight one-room apartments and seven ground floor retail stores facing the two streets. The evolution of the design explains in part the marked difference between the street facades and the rear patio elevation of the building which has a primitive vernacular starkness that one associates with the Pueblo Revival or with some buildings of Irving J. Gill. The only strong historic note is the curved portal with its Southwest adobe atmosphere of simple posts, stuccoed parapet and its groups of projecting vegas.

AS WAS USUALLY THE CASE WITH THIS ARCHITECT, the latest in technology was employed in the construction of the building. The frame was a combination of cast concrete members, referred to as "concrete lumber." These concrete framed walls supported thin (1 inch) concrete slabs. The concrete ornament was cast in reverse molds in place and was supported by bolts and wire.[71]

STACY-JUDD'S REFERENCES TO MAYA ARCHITECTURE were essentially an applique of decorative elements attached to the two street facades and within the public spaces of the hotel. The only pure Maya architectural feature he employed was the suggestion of a stepped temple platform posed at the street corner of the parapeted roof. A glance through the Catherwood plates in the Stephens volumes indicate where the architect obtained each of the specific motifs which he used."[72] As it is not entirely clear what the exact reason was for the peculiar medley of carved pieces, cubes and the many quaint shapes forming some of the Maya panels, I did not duplicate any particular original panel of the temples, but assembled the curious units to my own fancy."[73]

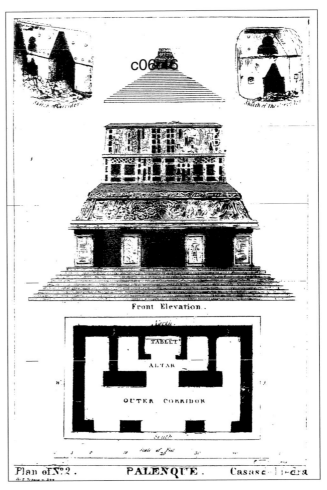

John L. Stephens, Incidents of Travel in Central America, Chiapas, and Yucatan. *(New York: Harper & Brothers, 1841); illustrations by Frederick Catherwood.*

BECAUSE OF ITS RELATIVELY LOW COST, cast concrete was the material used by Stacy-Judd for the ornament as well as for the external hanging lights. Because he was relying on the strong line drawings from the Stephen's volumes and because of the cost of making the wood forms, the ornament on the Aztec hotel was realized via projecting flat planes defined by sharp right angles. This transformation from the original source ended up in having two advantages: the designs have a slightly modern (almost Art Deco) quality about them, and the knife-edged patterns read effectively even on the rare non-sunny Monrovia day.

ORIGINALLY THE EXTERIOR "was stuccoed and finished in a green color, with a faint admixture of brown and blue, giving a general effect of sage green."[74] The architect's wish was to separate his stucco

"The Maya Lobby," La Jolla Beach & Yacht Club.

Renderings by Robert Stacy-Judd

right, Maya warrior. (A. Peres collection)
below, "The Destruction of Atlantis"

"Research, Hypothetical Study," utilizing ancient Maya art motifs.

Mayan bath, T.A. Willard residence, Beverly Hills.

Dr. Gale Atwater residence, Elysian Park, Los Angeles.

Lake Mead Recreational Area, Pierce Ferry, Arizona project.

Interior of the Maya Theatre (proposed).

"Streets of All Nations," Robert Stacy-Judd residence.

La Jolla Yacht & Beach Club.

City Block, Wilshire Boulevard, Los Angeles.

War Memorial, Minot, North Dakota (proposed)

Photographs by Anthony Peres

left, Mural, Aztec Hotel.
right, Lobby of the Aztec Hotel.

Aztec Hotel, Monrovia, California.

right, Pulpit, First Baptist Church.
below, Bas relief panels, First Baptist Church.
opposite, First Baptist Church, Ventura, California.

above, Soboba Hot Springs Resort, San Jacinto, California.
right, Tower detail, Soboba Hot Springs Resort.

54

right, Atwater Bungalows, second story stair-run.
below, Atwater Bungalows, showing
eucalyptus log porch.

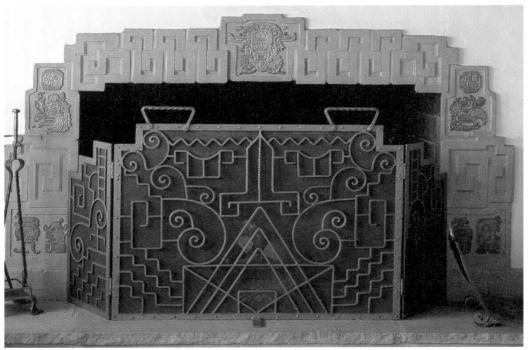

Mayan fireplace, Wise residence, Oceano, California.

Wise residence, Oceano, California.

Masonic Temple, North Hollywood, California.

Atwater Bungalows, view toward courtyard

building from the generally normal white stucco Spanish Colonial revival structures around, and also he wished to suggest an aged patina surface for his building.

THE INTERIOR WAS EVEN RICHER than the street facades in its references to the world of the Maya. Cast concrete again was used for ornament around entrances, the lobby fireplace, and the capitals of piers. "The stone [cast concrete] has been aged until it almost appears to have a patina, and its coloring a rich golden buff."[75] Color once again was of great importance, and the walls were "painted with a strong rich blue fading towards the ceiling."[76] The architect himself also painted (as Stacy-Judd often did) a number of the murals in the vestibule, the lobby and the dining room. He also laid out the stenciled designs used for the ceiling decoration and for the cast concrete and metal light fixtures. All of the principal wood and upholstered furniture decorated in reds, black and green, with appropriate Maya motifs was designed especially for the hotel. Some of it was designed by the architect, while the rest was obtained from Barker Brothers in Los Angeles. The general atmosphere of the public spaces is a mixture of Arts and Crafts, of the then-fashionable Southwest Pueblo Revival (a return to the folk and the "primitive"), countered by the historic richness of the Maya revival.

THERE WAS NO OTHER BUILDING CONSTRUCTED in Southern California at the time which reached such a degree of international and national notoriety. It was published in newspapers throughout the world, in low and highbrow magazines, and in professional and trade journals. The hotel was featured in several books, including the often cited volume, by Francis S. Onderdonk.[77] This fame was in no small part due to Stacy-Judd's adroit abilities in making sure his work was publicized. His years in England devoted in part to advertising and the

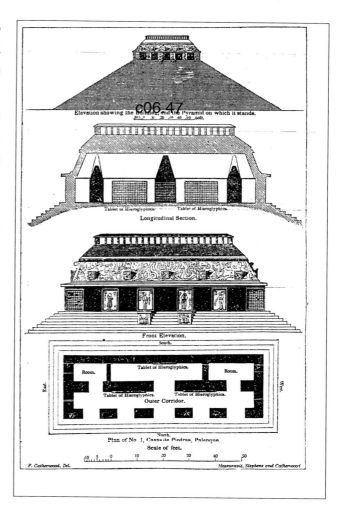

John L. Stephens, Incidents of Travel in Central America, Chiapas, and Yucatan. *(New York: Harper & Brothers, 1841); illustrations by Frederick Catherwood.*

59

merchandising of motion picture theaters prepared him well to deal with public relations in America in the twenties, and especially with Los Angeles and the promotional frenzy of the burgeoning motion picture industry. People in the twenties were in a mood to accept and be intrigued by the exotic, whether it was the opening of the tomb of Tutankhamen in Egypt, or the discovery of the "lost" cities of Yucatan and Central America. Thus, Stacy-Judd's exercise in the pre-Columbian came at the perfect moment, and he made the most of it.

THE AMUSING GUESSING AS TO WHO WAS FIRST with an idea is always a delightful game, but one which should not be taken too seriously. What has been claimed to be first at one moment in history has again and again been dethroned later by discovering something else was actually first. In the instance of the Aztec hotel, "the first building in the Maya style in the United States," fact should be separated from perception. Stacy-Judd's PR releases, in which he repeatedly made this assertion, were generally accepted as true whether they were or not. Writers and editors of the country's major newspapers and architectural journals had no qualms about broadcasting the building as the first in the Maya style.

Reactions to the Aztec Hotel

IN THE TWENTIES, at least, only a few were around who questioned Stacy-Judd's pioneering claim. The critic-historian Rexford Newcomb, from time to time, was uneasy about the quality of Stacy-Judd's designs, but he too asserted the firstness of Stacy-Judd and the Aztec Hotel. In 1927, he wrote the architect that "Your attack is an original one and you are to have all the credit that comes from originating something new and worthwhile."[78] On the other hand, when it came to the quality of design the editors of the *Western Architect* were not impressed: "Mr. Stacy-Judd's Aztec Hotel at Monrovia and his projects for hotels and residences are most astonishingly inept as to adaption and design, and irritating in character. They seemed to have been conceived to furnish irrefutable demonstration once and for all of the complete impossibility of the style for any modern purpose."[79]

EQUALLY UNIMPRESSED WITH STACY-JUDD'S EXERCISE in Maya architecture was the Southern California establishment architect, Carleton Monroe Winslow. He wrote with the Aztec Hotel specifically in mind that "The style, if it is a style, might be appropriate enough for a building dedicated to theatrical or moving picture purposes—one's mind can be twisted around to imagine it as a sort of permanent stage scenery to advertise the purpose of the building. That is excuse enough. Hollywood Boulevard has like examples of Chinese and Egyptian styles, not to mention others, which are delightful and that because they are appropriate to the purpose involved. Used in other ways, the Maya style seems just one more dissonant element added to our already overworked sense of sight. If a hotel, for instance, is in the Maya style just to be 'different' and to attract attention, the artistic standard of the building sinks to the level of a sign board and lays itself open to be judged accordingly."[80]

AN AWARENESS OF PRE-COLUMBIAN ART and architecture of Mexico and Central America upon the part of the American public and of architects had slowly been developing since the early 1890s. An extensive presentation of Maya art and architecture was made at the 1893 World Columbian Exposition in Chicago. In this exhibition was included a partial reconstruction of several Maya buildings including the Nunnery at Uxmal and the corbeled arched entrance from Labna.[81] Exhibitions of Maya and other pre-Columbian art and architecture was also presented at the 1900 Pan-American Exposition at Buffalo, and at the 1904 Louisiana Purchase Exposition in St. Louis. An even more extensive exhibition of Native American art of the American Southwest and of Mexico and Central American was to be seen at the 1915 Panama California Exposition in San Diego.[82]

Chapter 7

American Architect & Building News, *July 5, 1890, Aztec House; (project).*

THE EARLY POPULAR FASCINATION WITH the civilization of the Maya was also cultivated by travel books published in the nineteenth century. Certainly, John L. Stephens's two volumes of 1841 and 1844, with their enticing plates by Frederick Catherwood, laid the foundation for this interest. These volumes were followed by Claude J. D. Charnay's *The Ancient Cities of the New World: Being Voyages and Explorations in Mexico and Central America, 1857-1882 (1887),* and A. P. and A. C. Maudslay's *A Glimpse at Guatemala and Some Notes on the Ancient Monuments of Central America* (1899).[83]

FOR ARCHITECTS, DRAWINGS AND LATER photographs had been included from time to time in professional magazines. *The American Architect and Building News* published drawings of Maya architecture as early as 1886, and in 1898, this magazine published a group of photographs of the structures at Mitla.[84] In his often mentioned 1876 volume, *The Habitations of Man in All Ages* Eugene Viollet-le-Duc provided his readers with drawings which reconstruct several of the Maya buildings of Yucatan.[85] Another book well used by architects was by Auguste Choisy. In his 1899 volume, *Histoire de L'Architecture,* he illustrates in his wonderful isometric drawings Maya buildings from Labna, Palenque, Uxmal and Chichen Itza. Discussions and occasional illustrations of the pre-Columbian architecture of Meso-

Eugene Viollet-Le-Duc, The Habitation of Man in All Ages, *1876.*

America occur in most of the general histories of architecture, written from the late nineteenth century on through the twenties.[87]

FROM 1900 ON THROUGH THE EARLY 1920S the Maya archaeologist Sylvanus G. Morley wrote a number of popular well-illustrated articles on the ancient Maya published in the widely read National Geographic Magazine.[88] As early as 1919, archaeologist Herbert J. Spinden was arguing that Meso-American architecture could serve as the basis for a new "national art."[89] The second decade of the century witnessed the publication of a number of classics studies on Meso-American archaeology. Among these were Thomas A. Joyce, *Mexican Archeology;* Sylvanus G. Morley, *An Introduction to the Study of the Maya Hieroglyphs;* Herbert J. Spinden, *Ancient Civilizations of Mexico and Central America,*

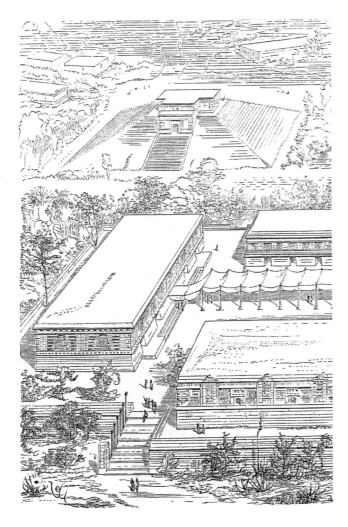

Eugene Viollet-Le-Duc, Ibid, *figure 87.*

as well as his *A Study of Maya Art.*[90] By the mid-twenties these and other volumes on Maya art and architecture found their way into private and institutional libraries across the country including, it should be noted, libraries of many architects.

Background of the Maya Revival

THE MID TO LATE TWENTIES WAS THE HEYDAY not only for an interest in Meso-American archaeology, but also for putting forth the idea that this Native American architecture could serve as a basis for a new "All-American" architecture.[91] The most often perused volume, in part because of its large illustrations, was George Oakley Totten's *Maya Architecture*.[92] By the early thirties these volumes were joined by Earl H. Morris's *The Temple of the Warriors at Chichen Itza,* and by additional articles published in the *National Geographic Magazine,* such as Sylvanus G. Morley's "Unearthing America's Ancient History," and "Yucatan, Home of the Gifted Maya."[93] As had occurred at earlier expositions, the public had an opportunity of experiencing a partial reconstruction of the famed Nunnery from Uxmal at the 1933 Century of Progress Exposition in Chicago.[94]

INTEREST IN PRE-COLUMBIAN ARCHITECTURE ART continued unabated through the 1930s and into the Post-World War II years. A match to Totten's well-illustrated volume was Tatiana Proskouriakoff's *An Album of Maya Architecture* with its series of her beautiful renderings.[95] Herbert J. Spinden continued to publish numerous popular and professional articles on the Maya, as did Frans Blom. The two classics on the Maya published in the years after 1945 were Sylvanus G. Morley's *The Ancient Maya* and J. Eric S. Thompson's *The Rise and Fall of Maya Civilization*.[96]

THE RATIONALE FOR THE USE OF ANCIENT MESO-AMERICAN architecture as a source for twentieth-century design was presented in an article on the 1912 Cordova Hotel in Los Angeles; "It was the desire on the part of the architects to incorporate in the building a style which would be distinctively American that led to the effort to apply to a modern structure the strange but interesting architectural ideas of the primitive Indian."[97]

THE MANY ARTICLES PUBLISHED in the twenties on the possibility of a Maya revival follow a repeated path. First, they asserted that American society was vastly different from Europe's and that our new society should develop its own architectural expression. New York architect Alfred C. Bossom (like Stacy-Judd, another English transplant) wrote, "We have no quarrel with the beauties of these types [the historical architectural styles of Europe], but so far do our ideals, our climate, and our temperament differ from those of Europe, that we can no longer continue to believe that these architectural importations express America.[98]"

THE NEXT STEP IN THE ARGUMENT WAS that since all architecture is in the end based upon historic precedent, America should seek a precedent within the New World as opposed to the old. As Herbert E. Angel wrote in 1930, the Native American sources which should be utilized are the Pueblo Architecture

Chapter 8

of the American Southwest and the pre-Columbian architectures of Meso-America.[99] Edgar Lloyd Hampton, who emerged as a major apologist for the Maya revival, summed it up in an article: "a new American culture is just on the eve of being born . . . . From a national standpoint this means that we presently shall have, in this country, an architecture and series of decorative principles that are a hundred percent American."[100]

STACY-JUDD HIMSELF ACKNOWLEDGED that others had preceded him in advocating that elements of Maya design (and designs derived from other pre-Columbian cultures) could provide a new basis for contemporary architecture. But he insisted that the Aztec Hotel was the first structure to use this style. "I am not," he wrote in 1964, "the first architect to realize the possibility of utilizing Ancient Maya Art motifs, but chance permitted me to be the first to complete such a structure."[101] He hedged his claim, by noting that his building was specifically based upon Maya architecture, not that of the Toltecs, the Aztec, or other Native American groups of Mexico and Central America.

WHAT WAS IN FACT THE FIRST TWENTIETH-CENTURY building to draw its imagery from the Maya and other pre-Columbian cultures of Meso-America? It was not the Aztec Hotel in Monrovia, though it is certainly true that it was Stacy-Judd's hotel which set the whole revival on its way. In the realm of unbuilt, projected buildings, there were the reconstruction of "Nahuan Palace" in Viollet-le-Duc's 1876 *The Habitations of Man in All Ages.*[102] In 1890 the *American Architect and*

Building News published a drawing entitled, "Aztec House," a design which was more Maya than Aztec.[103] Even by 1900, architects and those writing architectural history were showing that the pre-Columbian architecture of Meso-America could just as well serve as precedent for contemporary architecture as any other past architectural types.

TURNING TO ACTUAL BUILT BUILDINGS, certainly one of the first to clothe itself self-con-

sciously in this image was the previously mentioned four-story hotel in downtown Los Angeles, the Cordova Hotel.[104] This hotel was designed in 1912 by the Los Angeles architectural firm of Otto H. Neher and Chauncy F. Skilling (who, it should be noted, also owned the building). A 1913 advertisement for Atlas Portland Cement provided a drawing of the building and noted that "This beautiful building is the first adaptation of Aztec architecture to any modern building."[105] In this structure the architects scattered here and there on the two street facades stylized pre-Columbian masks and a few other details on what was essentially a simple reinforced concrete business block.[106] The decorative pre-Columbian details of the Cordova Hotel were derived from illustrations contained in a number of popular publications of the time including, of course, the *National Geographic Magazine.*

PREVIOUS TO THE CORDOVA HOTEL, segments of pre-Columbian art and sculpture were injected into a large well-published building, the Pan American Union in Washington, D.C. (1908-1910).[107] This impressive example of the Classical Beaux Arts tradition was designed by Paul Cret and Albert Kelsey. Into this Beaux Arts composition the architects injected elements from the Hispanic as well as the pre-Columbian Meso-American architectural traditions. We are told by George Oakley Totten that Albert Kelsey made two journeys to Yucatan to study the Maya style,

so it was probably Kelsey who was most likely involved in introducing these pre-Columbian elements into the building's design.[108]

E. S. Somers,. "Mayan Architecture and Its Modern Application," Architect and Engineer, *February 1931: Applications of Maya Details for a Modern Residence.*

THE REFERENCES IN THE PAN-AMERICAN UNION building to the architecture of the Maya are in a few decorative details. A stylized band exhibiting Maya motifs goes around much of the base of the building, and pre-Columbian motifs were utilized for the central patio pavement of the main building, for the sides of the shaft of the central fountain of the patio, and for many details on the Annex Building. References to Aztec and Toltec occur in many details and in "Aztec Garden," situated between the Main Building and the Annex.

IN THEIR USE OF THESE PRE-COLUMBIAN MOTIFS the architects "attempted to recall something of the mystery of that strange twilight time in American history which still baffles the savants of the world."[109]

ANOTHER EARLY EXAMPLE WHICH certainly must have been known to Stacy-Judd was the 1919-20 tunnel entrance to the Southwest Museum in Los Angeles. This fragment of the facade of a Maya Temple posed as a romantic ruin tucked into the wooded hillside. While the designers of this entrance, Allison and Allison of Los Angeles, looked primarily to the Maya architectural tradition of

Yucatan, they also borrowed freely from Mitla, the extensive Zapotec center situated near Oaxaca.[110] A far more grandiose project was toyed with by the Southwest Museum early in 1920. This was a proposal by the archaeologist Harold S. Gladwin and architect David C. Allison for a spectacular annex to the Southwest Museum consisting of a terraced forecourt leading up the hill to a new structure which appeared to be a complete Maya platform and temple.

THOUGH THE 1919 CLARK HOUSE in Santa Fe Springs, designed by California's early modernist, Irving J. Gill, incorporated Maya motifs, it may well have reflected his client's interest.[111] The concrete floor of the central patio contains free-form Maya glyphs, and within the patio, cast concrete planter boxes exhibit Maya-like high relief sculpture.

CONTEMPORANEOUS TO THE SUBWAY ADDITION to the Southwest Museum in Los Angeles and Gill's Clark house was a proposal in 1919, by the Washington D.C. architect George Oakley Totten for a new museum devoted to the Native Arts of the Americas.[112] It was noted that "The proposed building will be of a distinctly American character and will embody many features of the structures of Yucatan."[113] Totten had, in early 1919, traveled to Yucatan to visit many of the principal Maya sites. "It is the intention of Mr. Totten to reproduce the salient points of architectural beauty of the temple of the Tigers [at Chichen Itza].[114] Although the museum was never built, Totten became a great advocate of the Maya revival, publishing in popular magazines, and then, as noted, publishing his 1926 volume *Maya Architecture*.[115]

Gerhardt T. Krammer, "Maya Design," Architect and Engineer, 122, September, 1935: "Study for a Peace Palace for the Pan American Union," page 28.

Robert Stacy-Judd in Maya costume.

The Question of "Firstness"

During the time that Stacy-Judd's Aztec Hotel was receiving its wide recognition, another expatriate English architect, Alfred C. Bossom, emerged as a convert to the concept of employing pre-Columbian architecture of Meso-America for contemporary purposes.[116] Like Totten, Bossom traveled to Mexico and to the Yucatan. While there, he was actively involved in the proposals for the restoration of several of the temples at Tikal.[117] He took the theme of the high platform temples at Tikal as the inspiration for his example of the most acclaimed all-American building type of the twenties, the Skyscraper. Bossom's design for a skyscraper to have been located on Madison Ave. (c. 1926) takes the set-back theme of the twenties high rise and realizes it with vertical emphasis and elements of mass reminiscent of Art Deco. He introduces Maya ornament as a termination of each of the building's receding blocks and topped his building with a Maya stepped pyramid which recalls several of the temples at Tikal.[118]

Though Stacy-Judd, Alfred C. Bossom, Edgar Lloyd Hampton and others had hopefully predicted that the pre-Columbian of Meso-America would emerge as a new source for modern American architecture, this did not happen. Instead, American architects and their clients continued to look to Europe for the latest fashion, in the case of the late twenties and early thirties the Parisian-inspired Art Deco. Still, there was a smattering of examples of the pre-Columbian around the country, and certain Maya motifs were incorporated into the Art Deco itself. Two of these architectural features were the stepped corbel arch or vault and the stepped pyramid as the termination of the building.

The incorporation of pre-Columbian details into Art Deco buildings can vividly be seen in the entrance to the 535 feet tall Union Trust Building (now the Guardian Building), 1927-29 in Detroit.[119] Above the entrance arch an Aztec-like head poses between two extended wings, and within the semi-circular opening, three stepped corbel arches appear. Similar appliques of Maya and Aztec motifs occur in the entrance lobby of the Marine building in Vancouver (1930) and as occasional decorative motifs on the exterior of the 1930 Berkeley Public Library.[120]

In the realm of high art architecture the most sophisticated example of the incorporation of Maya motifs into the Art Deco/Streamline Moderne is to be found in the 1929-30 450 Sutter Street building in San Francisco, designed by Timothy Pflueger[121] (Miller and Pflueger). The Sutter Street building rendered Maya motifs in low relief in stone and in cast aluminum panels, all of which seem beautifully integrated into the over-all design of the building. Another, equally thoughtful use of the pre-Columbian occurred in the Luther Burbank Junior High School building (1929) in Los Angeles.[122]

Chapter 9

As Carleton Monroe Winslow had observed, the use of the exotic as a romantic and fanciful stage set for theaters was logical and appropriate.[123] The four most full-blown motion picture theaters in the pre-Columbian guise were the Mayan Theater in Los Angeles (1926-27), the Fisher Theater in Detroit (1928), the Mayan Theater (1929-30) in Denver, and the Aztec Theater (1926) in San Antonio. Both the Mayan Theater in Los Angeles, and the Fisher Theater in Detroit are not only rich and elaborate in their version of Maya architecture, but also entailed a complex conceptual program in their early planning stages. In the case of the Detroit theater the Maya archaeologist Sylvanus G. Morley was involved, and for the Los Angeles theater it was the artist, Francisco Cornejo.[124]

In addition to numerous commercial and even public buildings that incorporated Maya motifs in the decorative programs, some designs went one or two steps further in the use of the idiom. The interest in the exotic and remote may have prompted the architects or the client of the Elks Club in Aurora, Illinois (1926) to cloth portions of the buildings' exterior in terra cotta bands displaying Maya relief sculpture.[125] Several restaurant and hotel interiors during the late 1920s also played with the pre-Columbian theme. One of the most exuberant was the Aztec Room of the Hotel President in Kansas City and the more low-keyed Maya Room of the Madrillon Restaurant in Washington, D.C.[126]

The one designer who came closest to Stacy-Judd and his version of Maya architecture was the Beverly Hills architect Elbert S. Somers. In February, 1931, he published an article in the San Francisco-based *Architect and Engineer* entitled "Maya Architecture and Its Modern Application."[127] Somers illustrated his article with a number of his own designs he had derived from Maya architecture and relief sculpture. In addition there were drawings for a proposed "Civic Structure" and for a "Modern Residence." From the point of view of accomplished designs, these two proposed buildings are very successful in carrying out the Maya theme. It is regrettable that none of Somer's designs were apparently built.

In the mid to late twenties for pre-Columbian architecture was a similar enthusiasm in the decorative arts, particularly in ceramic tile.

Earnest Batchelder, the Pasadena tile designer, turned from his earlier Arts and Crafts themes to Maya motifs (along with Moorish and Spanish motifs) in the mid-1920s. Accompanying him in this adaptation of the pre-Columbian mode were a number of other tile manufacturers in Southern California: the California Clay Products Co. produced a line of tile called "Aztec," and the Malibu Tile Company illustrated a wonderful array of different Maya mantels (including andirons) in their catalogues.[128]

RUNNING PARALLEL TO THE OUT-AND-OUT effort to revive Maya architecture was the impact of this ancient architecture on a number of America's foremost avant-garde designers of the first three decades of the century. There were subtle innuendos of the pre-Columbian present in the monumental massing and fenestration of several of the pre-1911 designs by Walter Burley Griffin and Frank Lloyd Wright.[129] Wright's first effort to really abstract the Maya tradition was his 1915 German Warehouse in Richland Center, Wisconsin.[130] In this building he provided the classical, richly ornamented band at the top of his building which one finds in so many Maya buildings. The ornament itself, realized in cast concrete, probably was as much inspired by Maya ornament as by the Zapotecs.

THE INSPIRATION OF PRE-COLUMBIAN Meso-American design formed the romantic basis for all of his early work in Southern California starting with Aline Barnsdall's "Hollyhock House," of 1917-1921.[131] In the Alice Millard house of 1923, in Pasadena, Wright adapted his first full use of patterned concrete block. His approach to these block patterned walls is more a reflection of its use at the Zapotec structures at Mitla, than any Maya buildings. Of all of his twenties precast concrete block houses in California, it is the Charles Ennis house of 1924, which really does pose as an ancient pre-Columbian temple on top of its steep and precipitous hill. Wright also exported the pre-Columbian to the Midwest, and even further (and quite surprisingly) to his famed Imperial Hotel (1916-1922) in Tokyo, Japan.

WRIGHT'S ELDEST SON LLOYD WRIGHT also embraced the pre-Columbian Meso-American tradition in the 1920s. In his 1926 John Sowden house Lloyd Wright provided an interior courtyard with suggested temples at each end, accompanied by pairs of stela.[132] His most expansive version of the pre-Columbian was his projected Hotel and Bungalows (c. 1927-28) for Lake Arrowhead where he posed two stepped pyramids, between which occurs an elongated Maya temple articulated by repeated stepped corbel openings.[133]

Though Stacy-Judd did not mention any of these buildings by Lloyd Wright, Frank Lloyd Wright, and others in the L. A. scene, he surely must have been well aware of them. Equally, it is surprising that he made no comments on George Oakley Totten's beautifully illustrated volume on Maya architecture, although one suspects that he knew it well (and probably owned it), for a number of his post-1926, Maya-inspired designs resemble its illustrations. But such an omission on his part was one of the devices he continually employed to bring more emphasis to the originality of his own contributions. To have acknowledged these others might have watered down his claim of being the first architect to realize a Maya revival building in the country.

Stacy-Judd after the Aztec Hotel

THE INTRODUCTION OF THE MOTEL in Southern California was another claim to being first by Stacy-Judd. In 1924, he designed for the Hockenberry System the Motel O'Rodome at Beaumont.[134] While this two-story hostel faced onto two streets, its real entrance was via automobile through a Maya corbel arch entrance into an inner court, where the automobile was parked in front of one's room. For this projected motel, Stacy-Judd adapted the Pueblo Revival image, heightened by a scattering of Maya architectural and sculptural details.

IN HIS SCHEME FOR THE MAYA HOTEL (1925) at Tijuana, Mexico, he introduced even bolder assertions of the Maya image via corbeled openings and heavy projecting bands of sculpture at the top of the building. The entrance, with its inward curving walls, is indeed "organic," somewhat akin to a large loaf of bread, enlarged and rendered in cement stucco. Behind the entrance facade is a small rectangular tower which seems to hark back to the turn-of-the-century Mission Revival. Both of these projected hotels convey a rustic, primitive quality which one associates more with New Mexico's adobe tradition than with the pre-Columbian architecture of Meso-American.

OUT OF THIS AND OTHER VARIED MOTEL/HOTEL PROJECTS OF THE YEARS 1924-25 evolved his partially realized scheme for the La Jolla Beach and Yacht Club (1926-1927). In the brochure devoted to the Club, Stacy-Judd described the first unit as being of Maya architecture. However, Horace T. Major, a director of the club, characterized it as "of Spanish architecture" and "Mayan architecture will decorate the lobby of the club."[135] "Already magazines of international scope have arranged for interviews with Robert B. Stacy-Judd, Hollywood architect, whose brush and pen have conceived in this lobby a masterpiece of decoration and comfort. Gathering inspiration from Yucatan and Central America, Stacy-Judd has applied an ancient motif of decoration to a modern scheme of life."[136] The Maya stage set which he devised for the two-and-a-half-story lobby indeed was filled with Maya details; but regrettably this section of the project was never built. References to the Maya in the completed building were reserved for the dining room fireplace and some of the wrought-iron lighting.

AS FAR AS STACY-JUDD WAS CONCERNED, the small J. D. Carey house on Crescent Heights Boulevard was the "first attempt to utilize Maya motifs for domestic architecture."[137] His original proposal for the Carey house conveys the feeling of a nineteenth-century archaeological museum (a la Sir John Soane's house museum in London), a composition piled high with architectural fragments. It is as if the architect was determined to use every Maya motif he had ever come across in books and magazines: a V-shaped central window, accompanied by stelae, fountains and acres of scattered ornament. The house as finally built was far more reserved.

Chapter 10

The Maya details occurred as decorative devices on this building which was more Pueblo than Maya or Spanish.

WITH THE INTENSE ACTIVITY IN REAL ESTATE, and the creation of subdivisions, it should not be a surprise that Stacy-Judd was involved in a number of these schemes. One of these, Twin Lakes Park in Chatsworth (1927), was billed as the "Homesite of the Maya Village." Stacy-Judd designed and built a Tract Office which exhibited

Above: Motel O'Rodome, 1923-24, Beaumont; (project).
Below: La Jolla Yacht and Beach Club, La Jolla, general view, 1926-27.

his large diameter circular windows, placed within a wood and stucco volume which hints at the Maya. He projected a Maya style Gateway (in concrete), a Club house, and various "Aztec" type cabins. It was noted in the advertising brochure that all of the buildings to be erected at Twin Lakes Park should be in "the Maya or Southwestern" Indian

Above: La Jolla Beach and Yacht Club, La Jolla.
Below: Interior, La Jolla Beach and Yacht Club.

77

architecture, and that "an architectural board will advise and approve all designs for such structures."

ALONGSIDE THESE MAYA EXERCISES were a wide potpourri of images employed by the architect. These included Spanish Colonial Revival designs, such as the small John Chain house (1925) in Hollywood; versions of the Pueblo, the Worrell "Zuni House" (1926) in Santa Monica, and even the French Norman, in the Guy D. Sisson (1926) in Los Angeles.[138] For two of his larger projects of these years his clients requested that the design be within the Pueblo/Spanish tradition.

Above: John D. Carey House, 1927, Hollywood.
Below: Twin Lakes Park, Entrance, 1927, Chatsworth.

Such was the basis for design for the group of buildings he designed in 1924, for the Krotona Institute of Theosophy in Ojai, and for a group of speculative houses he produced for Merrick and Ruddick's subdivision in the eastern San Fernando Valley (1925). His catholic taste is well illustrated as suggested in the variety of house types he produced for another subdivision,

that of Beverly Ridge (1927-28). As the consulting architect for the Beverly Ridge Co., he depicted dwellings whose images ran from the Maya to the Pueblo, Spanish Colonial Revival, and variations on Irving J. Gill's puritanical white stucco volumes.[139]

AMONG STACY-JUDD'S PROJECTS OF THE 1920S, the only one which approached the notoriety in its publicity of the Aztec Hotel was his Indian Village and Hotel at Soboba Hot Springs (1924-1927), located near San Jacinto. "Architect Robert B. Stacy-Judd is a man of ideas and ideals," wrote Joe Minister in 1927, "to him came the thought of perpetuating in this one establishment, much of the antiquity of the Southwest Indian dwellings . . . Having dreamt this dream, the architect proceeded to study and research a lot. The lore of lost races and valiant tribes . . . have long been one of his real hobbies . . ."[140] Stacy-Judd remarked about his approach, "The architecture in these buildings is as nearly true expression of the impulse of the

Above: Twin Lakes Park, Tract Office, Chatsworth, 1927.
Below: John Chain House, 1925, Hollywood.

various tribes as it is possible for me to conceive, commencing with the igloo-shaped and squared sloping walls of the mound, continuing on to the tepee, and ranging thence through the various styles up to the hill settlement tribe and Cliff Dwellers. In one instance a slight Christian influence via the depiction of a cross is seen creeping into the design. This is to commemorate the invasion of the Spaniards."[141]

Above: Worrell House exterior, (Zuni House), 1926, Santa Monica.
Below: Worrell House interior.

THE ARCHITECT'S GRAND SCHEME FOR SOBOBA Hot Springs Hotel and Indian Village consisted of a three-story hotel and bath house at the foot of the steep hillside with some fifty cottages above, each supposedly expressing one or another of the major native groups of the west and southwest. The main hotel building was never realized, and only a dozen of the Indian cottages were built. The two cottages which attracted the most attention were the Pima

bungalow designed after the style of the tepee home built by that tribe and the Yuma cottage whose igloo styles "follows the type used by the Yuma tribe."[141]

Guy D. Sisson House, 1926, Los Angeles.

ALMOST ALWAYS, WHEN STACY-JUDD PLAYED with "primitive" forms, the resulting design belies the hand of a professional architect; instead it conveys the feeling of a do-it-yourself amateur. What he was thinking about when he designed bungalows symbolizing the architecture of the Pueblo Indians, the Maricopa, the Hopi and others is difficult to know. Even the Hopi bungalow, where he could have looked to the existing original buildings in northern Arizona bears no resemblance to the Mesa dwellings of these people. Into these designs he injected unbelievable phallic chimneys, strange plastered domes and roofs, and gigantic grossly over-scaled roof canales. The overall effect of these buildings at Soboba Hot Springs is one of improbability and playfulness. It is obvious from their initial success in drawing visitors, that

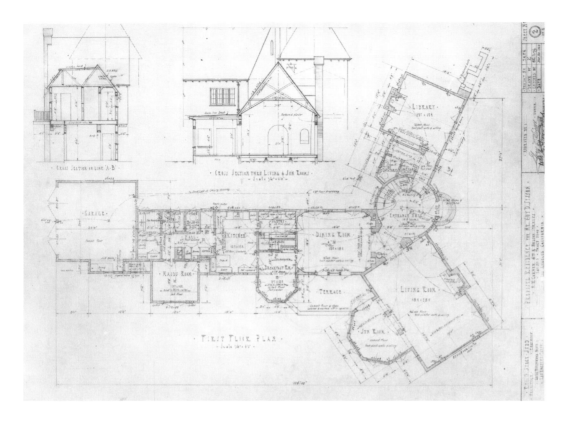

First floor plan for Guy D. Sisson House, Los Angeles, 1926.

Stacy-Judd had once again built something which appealed to a segment of Southern California taste.

AT THE END OF THE TWENTIES, Stacy-Judd received two commissions which enabled him to apply his Maya theme to large scale country and suburban houses. The first was the Neil E. Monroe house out in the country at Sherwood Forest (1929). "Originally," he wrote, "the design was prepared on a Spanish Theme. When the working drawings were almost completed the owners requested the design be changed to Maya motifs. To make the complete change meant discarding practically all of the working drawings, thereby incurring considerable additional expense. We compromised. I endeavored to blend motifs from the two styles."[143]

EXTERNALLY, A V-SHAPED MAYA OPENING was introduced into an essentially Spanish design. A central fountain wavers between being Maya and Art Deco. More outright Maya were such features as wrought iron lights and a metal cut-out weather vane depicting a Maya Priest renewing the fire of life. In the living room "The columns of the fireplace are replicas of a Mayan temple colonnade . . . the mantlepiece

duplicates a temple lintel . . . the windows narrowing at the top resemble a Maya arch. The friezes are replicas of Mayan temple carvings."[144]

THE SECOND OF THESE LARGE HOUSES was for his close friend and fellow Maya explorer, Theodore A. Willard (1929, 1932). The house enjoyed a prominent location, at the corner of Benedict Canyon Drive and Roxbury Drive. Willard's wish was to have a house which would reflect both the Maya and the moderne.[145] Except for its pro-

Above: Krotona Institute of Theosophy, 1924, Ojai.
Below: Krotona Institute of Theosophy, the Library.

nounced cornice, Stacy-Judd's design approached the cubist pose one associates with Irving J. Gill. Here and there within its plain concrete walls, the architect located Maya fragments. These were supplemented by textured block concrete walls, free standing stelae, and fountains. As in the Monroe house, the interior of the Willard house was rich in Maya detail, and somewhat bewildering in its play of scale, from monumental piers and lintels to delicate cast

and painted Maya glyphs. Though Stacy-Judd produced the complete working drawings for this house, it was never built.

Above and below: Merrick and Ruddick Housing Project, 1925, North Hollywood.

IN A MUCH SMALLER SCALE, Stacy-Judd illustrated how the Maya theme could be adapted to the small house. At Chatsworth in the San Fernando Valley he designed the Twin Lakes Model Maya Home (1927), and he made use of Maya motifs in the small beach cottage for William M. Wise in Pismo Beach (c. 1929). In these smaller designs Stacy-Judd suggested that we should react in two ways: with an awareness that they

are moderne, i.e. Art Deco and that they have deep historical roots via the use of Maya motifs. YET ANOTHER OF STACY-JUDD'S CLAIMED FIRSTS was the First Baptist Church in Ventura (1928-32). This was, according to the architect, the "First ecclesiastic structure embodying Maya motifs."[146] Though the Ventura church does encompass Maya motifs, its design is based upon the well-known and well-published contemporary Expressionist churches designed in Denmark by P. V. Jensen Klint. In his design for the Grundvig Church in Copenhagen (1913, 1921-1926), Jensen Klint had taken the form of the traditional Danish village church, with its combined tower and entrance facade, and had accentuated its verticality even more by thin perpendicular lines. The result read almost as an overscaled church organ with its ascending row of pipes. Similar "Gothic-spired" verticalism entered into the designs of several European and American Expressionist architects of the twenties and early thirties. The German architect Fritz Hoger's played the vertical theme in his Chilehaus in Hamburg (1923), and in America Bruce Goff and Barry Byrne both produced churches with attenuated vertical facades.[147] All of these Expressionist designs were published in American magazines. In addition to these buildings, this accentuated verticalism became one of the themes in the American Art Deco.

Above: Merrick and Ruddick Housing Project, 1925 North Hollywood.
Below: Beverly Ridge Development, 1927-28, Beverly Hills; (project).

Soboba Hot Springs Hotel "The Indian Village" 1924-27, San Jacinto.

Above and below: Soboba Hot Springs Hotel, "The Indian Village," 1924-27, San Jacinto.

THE MAYA THEME IN STACY-JUDD'S BAPTIST CHURCH occurs in the V-shaped openings, in projecting small pavilions which read almost as small temple-like forms. Maya motifs are also revealed in cast grille work, painted and stenciled patterns. For the pulpit, he outrageously had recourse to a Maya "sacrificial altar". Stacy-Judd repeated this vertical theme in a number of unbuilt projects of these years, including his proposed War Memorial, Minot, North Dakota (1927), the project for the Ixtapalapi Chapel near Mexico City (1932), and the projected Church of Jesus Christ of the Latter-Day Saints, Mexico City (1934). Thin vertical lines, in the manner of Hugh Ferriss, occur in his office tower contained in his proposal for two-blocks of building on Wilshire Boulevard, Los Angeles (1932).

Above and below: Neil E. Monroe house, 1929, Sherwood Forest, Ventura County; (photo: Donald Biddle Keyes).

STACY-JUDD WAS, AS HE HAD BEEN in other communities, socially involved in the community and the architectural profession in Los Angeles. "During the period of 1920 to 1930, Los Angeles became quite socially inclined. Among the many artistic and intellectual groups were the 'Round the World Club' and the Pacific Geographic Society, the later organization was formed in my office to gather and exchange knowledge covering the entire Pacific Literal."[148] In reading his autobiography, it is obvious that he was very much taken up with the Hollywood film crowd during those years: attending innumerable parties and dinners, going on overnight trips into the inland valleys and mountains, and voyages on friends' yachts off the California coast. While there is a degree of name-dropping in his autobiography, it would appear that he was continually a welcomed guest at many social affairs. He mentions such film personages as Jack Warner, Rex Ingham, Alice Terry, Milton Sills, Doris Kenyon, and others. "It was at the Standahl Gallery in Los Angeles," he wrote, "that Mr. Standahl introduced me to Bette Davis. She had expressed the wish because of her recent interest in the Ancient Maya civilization."[149]

STACY-JUDD BECAME A REGISTERED ARCHITECT in California in 1924, and a member of the American Institute of Architects in 1928. He was particularly active in the Architects League of Hollywood, authoring their publication *The Architect's Cost and Profit*.[150] In 1927, he presented three lectures at the Architects League of Hollywood, and

Neil Monroe Residence, 1929; Above:
Living Room interior;
Below: Dining Room interior.

Theodore A. Willard House, 1919-1932, Beverly Hills; (project).

these were gathered together and published under the title *Mayan Architecture—Its Adaptability to Modern Conditions.*[151] The "Personal and Trade Notes" of the August 13, 1926 issue of the Southwest Builder and Contractor noted that "Architect Robert B. Stacy-Judd will entertain the members of the Architects' League of Hollywood with an Aztec dinner at the Aztec Hotel, Monrovia at 7:15 p.m., Aug. 26."[152] One can only conjecture as to what Stacy-Judd thought an Aztec dinner might consist of. Perhaps, at affairs such as this, he may have entertained his guests costumed as he occasionally was as a Maya priest-king.

ON JUNE 29, 1925, STACY-JUDD and three friends stayed overnight in Santa Barbara. Early the following morning this coastal city experienced its devastating earthquake.

IN HIS USUAL HIGHLY DRAMATIC FASHION, he related his experience in Santa Barbara. "At 6:45 the next morning, while I was shaving, the three-story hotel began to sway, rhythmically, back and forth . . . I counted eight such movements, a few seconds apart. A few minutes later a very hard shock was felt. Again, the building began a series of sickening sways. At the same time, I heard buildings crashing into the street . . . I finished shaving, packed my bags and hurried down the shaky and groaning staircase to the lobby. Somebody in the street caught sight of me and shouted 'Get the hell out of there. She's going to fall.' I was the last to leave."[153] In a fashion akin to a B-rated Hollywood film, he related how he rescued an elderly woman: "Jumping from the car I

First Baptist Church, 1928-32, Ventura.

First Baptist Church, Ventura.

started towards the woman. At that moment the entire earth area, including the front lawn, from the street to the house, suddenly opened up, forming a succession of small islands, each isolated by wide and deep crevasses . . . . I jumped from one 'island' patch to the next, hastening to the woman on the porch. She continued to scream as I pulled her onto the moving earth. We jumped from one miniature island to another, each time barely missing a fall into spaces between. Considering our hasty flight, it is miraculous how we escaped."[154] Upon returning to Los Angeles he prepared a report for the Architects League of Hollywood on why various buildings did not survive the earthquake—usually because of their poor masonry construction.[155] He also wrote up his earthquake experience in Santa Barbara for publication, but this was never published.

Above: Exterior detail, First Baptist Church, Ventura.
Below: First Baptist Church, interior.

The Architect as Jungle Explorer

IN THE MID-1920S, STACY-JUDD had met Theodore Arthur Willard, president of the Willard Battery Company. Willard had invented his highly successful version of the storage battery and had established a profitable manufacturing facility in Cleveland, Ohio. He moved to California in the twenties, but kept control of his company until he finally retired in 1936. Willard was one of Southern California's small band of devoted Maya enthusiasts, along with Rupert Hughes, author of *The War of the Maya Kings,* journalist Edna Robb Webster, and others.[156] Willard had already journeyed to Mexico and Yucatan, and in 1926, he had published his *The City of the Sacred Well.* He had followed this by four other publications, including a novel, *The Wizard of Zacna,* and another travel book, *Kukulcan, the Bearded Conqueror.*[157]

IN A LETTER TO MS. WEBSTER, DATED OCTOBER 28, 1929, Stacy-Judd set down his elaborate goals for the trip to Yucatan, "As you realize I am exceedingly keen on exploring the areas occupied by the first and second known Maya dynasties, and with this urge ever in mind I conceived the idea of organizing a fully equipped expedition into the area of the early Maya ruins. I sold the idea to Mr. Willard and have managed to secure a correspondent with expedition experience and a business manager who is a prominent publicity man in the west. The company will be known as the 'Willard, Stacy-Judd Maya Expedition' . . . I plan this expedition to be the largest to enter the Maya area."[158]

FOR A VARIETY OF REASONS, financial being the paramount one, Stacy-Judd had to pare down this grandiose expedition, but notwithstanding the beginnings of the Great Depression, it did take place. He and the Willards traveled by train to New Orleans, and then left by boat for Progreso on the Yucatan coast on the February 14, 1930. "I am taking a movie camera and about two thousand feet of film and a still camera with approximately twelve dozen negatives, so that I hope to come back with an interesting record of the trip. I am proposing taking voluminous notes with the object of building up a travelogue story and numerous articles upon my return."[159]

AS STACY-JUDD'S CORRESPONDENCE WITH EDNA ROBB WEBSTER indicates (she accompanied Willard on this 1930 expedition to Yucatan), he did not wish it to appear that he was a mere appendage to Willard. In December 1930, Ms. Webster prepared a story for national usage on the expedition labeled the adventure, "The T.A. Willard 1930 Expedition to Yucatan."[160] When Stacy-Judd saw this text he fired off a telegram, "Statement that Willard led expedition incorrect and will do me harm as it contradicts my book and articles. I journeyed with Willard to Merida and led my own expedition into the jungles at my own expense."[161] A few days later he wrote to Ms. Webster, ". . . the wonderful time I spend in Yucatan

Chapter 11

was primarily due to Mr. Willard's influence, which I freely and publicly acknowledge, but my adventures are my own and form the meat of my book and articles."[162]

STACY-JUDD'S 1930 TRIP TO YUCATAN encompassed four and a half months. He spent the first weeks with Willard in and around Merida, visiting Chichen Itza, Coba, Mayapan and other nearby Maya sites. While there he spent time with three of the most famed of the Maya archaeologists: Herbert Spinden of the American Museum of Natural History, Frans Blom of the Department of Middle American Research, and Sylvanus G. Morley of the Carnegie Institution. He took several long trips, of which one was to Uxmal along with Frans Blom. On a trip of his own he "discovered" the Caves of Loltun near Labna.

WITH HIS SIXTEEN MM. CAMERA, Stacy-Judd took several thousand feet of film, which he organized into two long presentations after he returned home. He also returned with numerous black and white photographs, as well as film which could be used for slide purposes. Though he talked of making detailed drawings and of taking notes on the architecture, his archives do not possess such material. One suspects that he ended up making notes for his book and articles, taking motion picture and still films, and that was it.

THE UNDERLYING GOAL OF STACY-JUDD'S Maya expedition was to advance his stature as a person knowledgeable about Maya archaeology

The El Castillo, Chichen Itza; (photo by Anthony Peres, 1993).

and architecture. This was more than adequately realized. He began lecturing around the Southland and showing his films. "Mr. Stacy-Judd is being importuned to publicly exhibit his remarkable pictures of the Maya architectural accomplishments in this little known land of Yucatan, and the first of a series of moving picture lectures will be given, commencing October 3 [1930] at the Los Angeles University Club. He has already arranged to give a number of exhibitions in many parts of the west because of the widespread interest that is being manifested in the subject."[163]

IN 1932, STACY-JUDD SUBMITTED HIS Maya manuscript to the New York publishing house of Bobbs-Merrill Co, but it was not accepted. Eventually, he had it published locally in Los Angeles in 1935, by Haskell-Travers, Inc.[164] It was entitled *The Ancient Maya,* and the illustration

The Nunnery Quadrangle, Uxmal; (photo by Robert Stacy-Judd, 1930).

opposite the title page was a photograph of our architect-explorer in his jungle costume replete with a belted revolver and machete. It was an adventure book and only incidentally was concerned with Maya archaeology and architecture. The dust-jacket for Kabah, the 1951 edition of the book sets forth the author's approach, "Mr. Stacy-Judd has departed from the usual textbook method of disseminating facts. He exposes the ruthlessness of the Jungle in attempting to hide from prying eyes the glories of the architectural achievements of the Ancient Mayas. In a style as gripping as the intriguing mystery story, historical facts become entertaining under the genius of this author's pen."[165]

BETWEEN OCTOBER 1933 AND FEBRUARY 1934, Stacy-Judd published a series of five articles on Maya architecture and its possibilities for adaption to modern architecture, in the California based magazine, *Architect and Engineer.*[166] He set the scene by the title of the first of the series, "Wanted—An All-American Architecture," and he concluded the series with "Some Local Examples of Maya Adaptations." All of the "Modern Adaptations" designs contained in the series are by Stacy-Judd. Continuing his personal self-promotionalism, he never really acknowledged that anyone else had ever designed Maya revivalist buildings. In the announcement of the series (including, of course, a photograph of Stacy-Judd in his pith helmet), he mentioned that he would be spinning off two books based in part on these articles. "The photographs and drawings which will accompany Mr. Stacy-Judd's articles are copyrighted and will be published also in a book now awaiting publication in New York. The book *Exploring Mysterious Yucatan* has already been accepted by one of the large eastern publishing houses."[167] But as was true of several of his other literary projects, this one never came to fruition. There is no question that the publication of these five well-illustrated articles helped to solidify his mixed reputation on the West Coast as a popular authority on Maya architecture, as well as being a quirky person and designer.

NEVERTHELESS, THERE WERE A FEW DISSENTING VOICES. A brief notice in the August issue of *Architect and Engineer* noted, "It seems that some authorities differ with Robert B. Stacy-Judd in his opinions." One of these was Gerhardt T. Krammer, an Associate in Architecture at the Department of Middle American Research at Tulane University. "I feel," wrote Krammer, "that the architectural profession should be interested in having a correct and archaeological side of the question presented."[168] In his article which followed, Krammer was obviously unhappy with such assertions by Stacy-Judd that the "earliest Egyptians were Maya Colonists," "that Christ was a Master of the Maya tongue and esoteric lore," and "that Christ's last words were pure Maya and possess a more ennobling meaning than the Biblical definition."[169]

KRAMMER ALSO HAD RESERVATIONS ABOUT the quality of design and the approach which Stacy-Judd took in the use of Maya ornament and forms. "Particularly in the West–Hotels, country clubs and yacht-club buildings, as well as theaters and even homes have been built in this [Maya] style, or rather claim to be representative of this style because of the weirdness of their designs. In most cases, however, the adaptation has been very unsuccessful and in many cases should not and justly cannot be called Maya."[170] Krammer then went on to zero in on Stacy-Judd's work. "Ornament, neither Maya nor Mexican in either feeling or character, has been unscrupulously strewn over the

Labná Arch, Yucatan.

wall surfaces of the building [the Aztec Hotel]. On the exterior of the Aztec Hotel in Monrovia, California, an assortment of scrolls have been tossed together and placed on bare wall surfaces where decoration was thought necessary. The designer has failed utterly in interpreting the symbolism or the craftsmanship of the original."[171]

STACY-JUDD WAS PROVIDED WITH an opportunity of replying to his critic.[172] He begins his retort by implying that Krammer is out to sell his own version of the Maya Revival, via the publication of his own scheme for a Peace Palace for the Pan American Union. Stacy-Judd then went on to say that one should not attack his first exercise in the Maya revival, the Aztec Hotel, for this design "was purely an experiment, and that at the time I designed the structure I knew practically nothing concerning the symbolic meaning of Maya motifs."[173] But having said this, he then went on to quote a number of "recognized authorities," Totten, Bossom, Newcomb, who had responded very positively to its design. His argument then goes on to indicate that Krammer is not competent to judge contemporary architecture: "I feel that Professor Krammer's inexperience in the practical field of architecture has led him to speak too hastily."[174] Finally he rejected in an ex-cathedra fashion, ". . . that Maya art was born, flourished, and died in Central America, or any parts of the Americas, is, in my opinion, without foundation."[175] "When it comes to the question of interpreting Maya symbolism, of which the Professor infers I am ignorant, I must ask his indulgence until my 'Atlantis, Mother of Empires' is off the press."[176]

HAVING EXPERIENCED THE EXCITEMENT of his first trip to Yucatan, Stacy-Judd drew up even more elaborate plans in 1932 for a second expedition, an expedition that was to have all the atmosphere of a major Hollywood film production. "This was intended to be," he wrote, "on a rather large scale. The personnel was to consist of a field staff of twenty-six scientists of various interests, a field engineer, a sculptor and clay modelers, camera men, a doctor, radio expert, aviator, public relations counselor and camp workers. A $400,000 corporation was formed . . . . The project included establishing a radio transmitting station at the jungle camp base for a period of three months. It was intended to transmit nightly nation-wide programs describing discoveries, adventures, and general activities gathered daily from a score of outlying posts in the jungle via portable transmitters to the base camp. Motion pictures were to record the activities of the expedition, and arrangements had been made for the sale of newspaper and magazine stories" on the part of Stacy-Judd.[177]

AS PART OF HIS PROPOSAL STACY-JUDD asked Maya archaeologist Frans Blom to join him and to reconstruct one of the buildings at Uxmal. Blom gently refused, for he was apprehensive about the architect. He had already met Stacy-Judd in Yucatan and sensed that he was primarily interested in advertising himself and his Maya revival architecture. With his retiring nature Blom was not at all interested in the "noisy advertising and ballyhoo" which he felt would result from the grandiose expedition.[178]

STACY-JUDD WENT TO MEXICO CITY to obtain the needed permits for this ambitious project. He visited a wide variety of Mexican governmental officials, finally discussing his project with Abelardo Rodrigues, President of Mexico. Stacy-Judd returned to the United States to complete his arrangements, but the project was finally

Robert B. Stacy-Judd traveling in Yucatan, 1930.

dropped "with the collapse of the country's monetary system, followed by the disastrous Southern California earthquake."[179]

AT THE TIME HE WAS ATTEMPTING TO ORGANIZE his second expedition, he married Betty Schofield on February 12, 1932, in his own First Baptist Church in Ventura. She was an artist and shared his interest in the Maya civilization. Though his expedition did not materialize, he and his wife did manage, in the mid and late thirties, to visit various pre-Columbian sites in the Valley of Mexico, at Mitla and other sites near Oaxaca. He mentions trips to Guatemala, but we do not know for sure whether he experienced such major Maya sites as Copan or Tikal, nor whether he experienced the important Maya site of Palenque.[180]

Philosophical Research Society building, 1935-37, Los Angeles.

Stacy-Judd in the Thirties

AS WITH MOST OTHER ARCHITECTS during the Depression years of the 1930s, Stacy-Judd experienced a marked decline in the number of his realized commissions. Between 1930 and 1932, he submitted three grand scaled proposals for city blocks in Los Angeles. "As it happened all three suffered total abandonment, or at least postponement, through the recent depression."[181] The first of these for the Wilshire (Tatum) block on Wilshire Boulevard (1930-31) was a single monumental building covering an entire city block. The project included stores, offices, a theater and other uses. The plan was in the form of a cruciform, and "The Maya form used is the stepped pyramid. An elevated sidewalk, twenty feet wide, serves an upper row of stores in the front facade."[182] As was the case with his First Baptist Church in Ventura, both the quality of the Art Deco as well as Expressionism is revealed in this design capped, of course, by references to Maya architecture.

HIS OTHER TWO EARLY THIRTIES URBAN PROJECTS were the Fox Group buildings (1931) on Wilshire Boulevard and the Paramount Group (National Hall Project, 1931) at the corner of Sunset and Vine. The Paramount group was set on two city blocks, with each of its components reading as separate buildings. These components consisted of a 23,000 seat auditorium, a thirteen-story department store, an office block, a hotel and a 2,500 seat theater. "Among the interesting features are the tower top of the office block, which shows the so-called Maya 'arch' as the motif for the silhouette . . ."[183] The Fox Block is somewhat similar, only the vertical pleated walls with their expressionist overtones are more pronounced. The most dramatic feature of the design is the sign for the Fox Theater, where vertical projecting walls exhibit rich Maya ornament. Even the letters on the sign are stepped in a Maya fashion.

OTHER UNREALIZED LARGE SCALE PROJECTS of the thirties were his complex for the Philosophical Research Society (1935-57) in Los Angeles, his "Streets of All Nations" project (1938) in Los Angeles, and his three Lake Mead resorts, one near Boulder City, Nevada, another for Pierce's Ferry, Arizona, and the last for The Lost City, Overton, Nevada (1938-1942).

"THE ARCHITECTURAL THEME FOR THE BUILDINGS of the Philosophical Research Society derives its inspiration from an outstanding, early culture of the American continent, that of the ancient Mayas."[184] In Manly Palmer Hall, the founder and president of the Philosophical Research Society, Stacy-Judd encountered the perfect client. Like Stacy-Judd, Hall was an aggressive salesman of his occult ideas, including his shared belief with Stacy-Judd in the existence and influence of the lost continent of Atlantis.[185] He also wrote on such diverse subjects as *The Mysteries of Electricity: A Retrospective and a Prophecy* and *Francis Bacon, the Concealed Poet*.[186]

Chapter 12

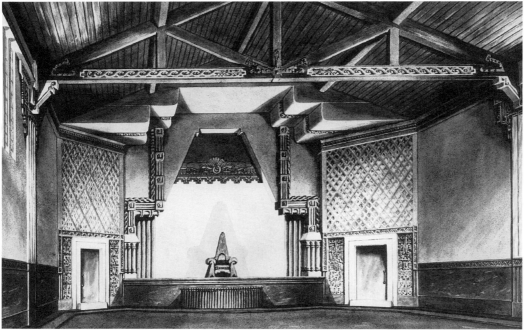

*Above: General View, and below: Lecture Hall, Philosophical
Research Society buildings, 1935-37, Los Angeles; (project).*

104

Streets of All Nations, proposed residence , 1938, Los Angeles.

THE STREETS OF ALL NATIONS project also had an occult flavor, mixed with commercialism. As theme architecture it was in certain ways similar to Robert V. Derrah's much smaller Crossroads of the World (1936) on Sunset Boulevard in Hollywood. The overall atmosphere of the project, its varied images, scale, street oriented scenes is obviously quite similar to Post-World War II Disneyland in Anaheim (1955 and later). Each of the major nations and cultures were to be represented by their own regional architectural image. A separate section of streets and courtyards was set aside for the display and sale of international arts and crafts. Within the project were restaurants, motels, motion picture theaters, churches and temples.

IT WAS A PERFECT PROJECT FOR STACY-JUDD, for here he could play with every world architectural image, and he did. China, India, Russia, England, France, Spain, Italy, North Africa were all represented. So too Native Americans, in the form of Pueblo and pre-Columbian architecture from Meso-America. The visually dominant buildings of the complex were the towering International Temple, the centrally placed Museum and Art Gallery, and a large hotel. These three buildings utilized Stacy-Judd's version of the Maya, mixed design elements derived from the Art Deco and late Expressionism architecture.

Above: Streets of All Nations proposed residence living room, 1938, Los Angeles.
Below: Streets of All Nations, proposed residence patio.

TWO SURPRISES AMONG THE DESIGNS are the central hotel which has a modernist image and the residence of the General Manager. In the manager's residence, Stacy-Judd did just what his critic Gerhardt T. Krammer had suggested, "Disrobed of their ornament, Yucatan Maya buildings are quite simple and hence easily should be adaptable to the temperament prevailing at present, which is towards simplicity." One can employ "the Yucatan Maya in its simplest form and using it distinctly in a modern building while still retaining the modernism in the massing and proportions of the building.[187] If one's aesthetic criteria is that of a traditionally proportioned and fenestrated building, rather than the openly exciting and at times delightfully bizarre, then his General Manager's house at the Streets of All Nations is his most sophisticated version of the Maya style modernized. (Stacy-Judd also employed this same design for a proposed residence for himself, 1936.)

Lost City Resort, 1938-42, Lake Mead Recreational Area, Overton, Nevada; (project).

Only parts of the complex were built over a period of some twenty plus years. The design is loosely Maya but quite simplified, almost modern in places. The most pronounced element of the design, the six-story entrance tower was a full-fledged Maya assertion, topped with stepped pyramid, composed of slope surfaces. The entrance hall within the tower would have been a two-story space with a V-shaped Maya vault. Also unbuilt were the Maya decorated lounge and lecture auditorium.

IN THE SUMMER OF 1938, Stacy-Judd was contacted by the Grand Canyon Boulder Dam Inc. to design a group of resorts on Lake Mead which had been formed behind Hoover (Boulder) Dam. Originally, three resorts were planned, eventually he was asked to design two additional resorts on the lake. "The problem," he wrote, "was to design three distinct resort centers, comprising a lodge and a number of cottages and other types of buildings, including all that goes to make a complete village . . . . The historical background of each location called for distinctive architectural treatment and in consequence necessitated widely different planning."[188]

FOR THE CENTRAL BUILDING at Boulder Beach Resort he looked back to the Spanish Colonial Revival of the 1920s, and even further back to the Mission Revival at the turn of the century. These Mission

Manager's House, Streets of All Nations, (also illustrated as house for Stacy-Judd), 1938, Los Angeles; (project).

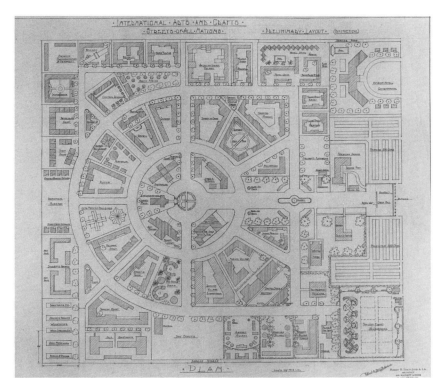

Project site plan of the Streets of All Nations, 1938.

and Spanish forms were, as one generally finds in the 1930s, highly simplified, similar in many ways to Cliff May's version of the California Ranch House. As a sales device he prepared his usual vividly colored drawings, plus a large model. The single and grouped cottages at Boulder Beach Resort were mildly Colonialized interpretations of the then popular California ranch house.

IN STRONG CONTRAST, the principal buildings and the cottages at Pierce's Ferry and at Lost City are clothed in Stacy-Judd's peculiar version of the Pueblo Revival. He treated the parapets of the buildings at Pierce's Ferry with a wildly undulating silhouette while doors, windows and openings for the loggia employed the V-shaped Maya arch, or strangely conceived curved openings. His Pueblo Revival buildings at Lost City seemly hark back to several of his designs at Soboba Hot Springs. The Lost City buildings all have walls which are battered in towards the top. They have the visual feel of being abbreviated tepees shorn of their tops. When he approached the edge of the lake at Pierce's Ferry, he radically shifted images and produced lukewarm modernist buildings with flat roofs and corner windows.

Church of Latter Day Saints, 1934, Mexico City, Mexico; (project).

WHILE STACY-JUDD ALWAYS WISHED to convey the image that he was a practical person, he seems also to find himself continually taken in by speculators and others. The project for the Lake Mead resorts entailed just the sort of grandioseness which appealed to him, but it was obvious from the start that the financing of this scheme was questionable. His various letters written between 1938 and 1941 indicated that he was taken for a ride and that he was never adequately paid for his work on this project. In commenting on this project in later life, he said that it was abandoned because of the Second World War. But his own correspondence indicates that the reason that the Lake Mead project was never built was in fact the shakiness of the company and its inability to raise the needed capital.

EQUALLY DISAPPOINTING WERE SEVERAL CHURCHES which he designed in the 1930s. None of them were ever constructed. The wildest of these was his proposed Chapel at Ixtapalapi, Mexico (1932), which takes the Art Deco, Expressionist scheme, enriched with Maya detail, and thrusts the whole composition vertically into the sky. Cast concrete Maya ornament surrounds the T-shaped entrance, and the central tower is climaxed by a Maya temple platform. Also, working

from the design theme of the First Baptist Church of Ventura was his scheme for the Church of Jesus Christ of Latter-Day Saints in Mexico City. If this church had been built, it would have been similar to his partially realized buildings for the Philosophical Research Society in Los Angeles.

OF THE FEW ACTUAL COMMISSIONS which Stacy-Judd saw built, the most exciting and "way-out" was his "Indian Village" for Dr. Gale Atwater (1930-31) in the hills of Elysian Park, Los Angeles. For the design of this group of bungalows he turned to the Pueblo Revival. There is a surrealist atmosphere to this design, with its undulating parapets (as if they have been subjected to natural forces over many years), ceramic pots placed on the corners of the parapets, oversized wood drain spouts, projecting wood balconies and rows of vegas, and wood ladders placed hither and yon on the flat roof. As shown in his presentation drawing equally wild non-native vegetation, palms, Italian cypress, and brilliant flowering shrubs, helped to make the building itself even more unreal.

Gale Atwater bungalows, "Indian Village," 1930-31 Elysian Park, Los Angeles, (photo by Anthony Peres, 1993).

111

John Clark House, 1939-41, Burbank.

His commissions for single family houses in the late thirties and early forties are all far more sedate than the Atwater "Indian Village." The Roland Dressel house (c. 1937) in Chatsworth and the Neil Monroe house (c. 1937) in San Bonito are simple unassuming versions of the single floor California Ranch House. Some of these house looked towards the moderne, such as the John Clark house (1939-41) at Burbank, with its simple unadorned stuccoed volumes, and horizontal metal corner windows. None of these houses are particularly strong or individual in their design. If one ran across them then or today, one would respond to them as typical of the time, and that is all.

With the general lack of commissions during the Depression years Stacy-Judd turned much of his energies to another somewhat wild, major research and writing project. This was a new look at the subject of the lost continent of Atlantis and the Maya as the principal descendants of this "lost race." This was a theme which had intrigued him from the moment of his first introduction to the architecture and civilization of the Maya.

At the conclusion of his two-volume work of 1841, John L. Stephens had concluded that the ruins which he and Catherwood had visited were not the work of migrant Egyptians or some other

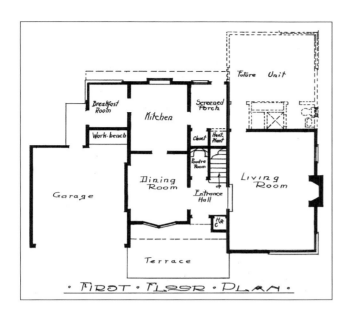

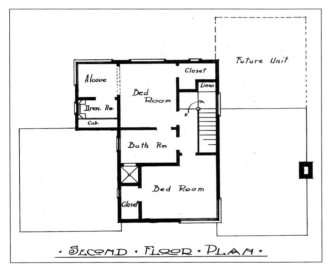

Above: First floor plan; Below: Second floor plan, John Clark House, 1939-41.

mysterious people, rather the ruins which they encountered ". . . were constructed by the race who occupied the country at the time of the invasion of the Spanish, or of some not very distant progenitors."[189] For Stacy-Judd this was too prosaic an answer to the question of the origin of the Maya civilization. His romantically imaginative temperament demanded an explanation which was not only romantic, but esoteric and dramatic as well.

Illustration: "Destruction of Atlantis," (detail).

The Myth of Atlantis

SOMETIME IN THE EARLY TWENTIES STACY-JUDD had picked up a book at a used book store in Los Angeles. This was the 490 page volume *Atlantis: The Antediluvian World,* authored by the Midwest populist, Ignatius Donnelly in 1882.[190]As was true with his contemporary Manley Hall, Ignatius Donnelly was in many ways a nineteenth-century personification of Stacy-Judd, at least in his continual advocacy of wild and extravagant ideas.[191] Donnelly (who was a lawyer, not a scientist or literary personage) not only became attached to the Atlantis myth, but he staunchly believed that Francis Bacon was the author of the plays and poems "mistakenly" associated with the name William Shakespeare.[192]

LIKE ALL ADVOCATES OF THE EXISTENCE OF ATLANTIS, Donnelly turned back to Plato's tale of Atlantis "Now in this island of the Atlantis," the Greek philosopher had written, "there was a great and wonderful empire which had rule over the whole island, and several others as well . . . . But afterwards there occurred violent earthquakes and floods; and in a single day and night of rain warlike men in a body sank into the earth, and the island of Atlantis in like manner disappeared and was sunk beneath the sea."[193] Plato went on in his discussions with Critias to describe in some detail the civilization and especially the architecture of Atlantis.[194]

IN HIS IMPRESSIVE VOLUME (336 PAGES) *ATLANTIS: The Antediluvian World,* Donnelly took as authority the factual truth of Plato's tale, and then he added his own twist that the pre-Columbian civilizations of Meso-America were one of several groups of colonist that had been sent out or had survived the destruction of Atlantis. " . . . all the traditions of Central America and Mexico point to some country of the East, and beyond the sea, as the source of their first civilized people; and this region known among them as 'Aztlan,' lived in the memory of the people . . ." and this land to the east was, of course, Atlantis.[195] In his advocacy of Atlantis as the source for Maya civilization, he joined a few others involved with the Maya, particularly the British explorer Frederick A. Mitchell-Hedges, and the theosophist turned Maya epigraphist William E. Gates.[196] As one would expect of the scientific community, all of the principal professional archaeologists involved with the study of the ancient Maya completely rejected the idea that the Maya civilization originated outside of Yucatan and the highlands.

IN HIS IMPRESSIVE *ATLANTIS—MOTHER OF EMPIRES* (1939) Stacy-Judd concurred with Donnelly "That there once existed in the Atlantic Ocean, opposite the mouth of the Mediterranean Sea, a large island, which was a remnant of an Atlantic continent, and known to the ancient world as Atlantis . . . That Atlantis was the region where man first rose from the state of barbarism to civilization . . . that Atlantis had

Chapter 13

sent out colonies in various directions, and that Atlantis perished in a terrible convulsion of nature, in which the whole island sunk into the ocean, with nearly all its inhabitants."[197] Where Stacy-Judd disagreed with Donnelly was the question of the location of Atlantis's first colony. For Donnelly, this was ancient Egypt, for Stacy-Judd it was the Maya of Yucatan. The Maya, wrote Stacy-Judd, were the ". . . direct race-child of the Mother of Empires, a root race of Atlantis."[198]

THE ROMANTIC THEORY OF A LOST ATLANTIS and that the Maya were colonists from it was a central theme of many late nineteen-century writers including such popular figures as Jules Verne.[199] The French explorer Augustus Le Plongeon carried this theme on with a twist, that the Maya were the chief colonists from Atlantis, and they in turn colonized much of the Mediterranean world, including Egypt. Le Plongeon's fanciful theory, advocated in his book, *Queen Moo and the Egyptian Sphinx,* was that the Maya civilization was derived from Atlantis and that the Maya Queen Moo crossed the Atlantic and joined "the Maya colonist which for many years had been established on the banks of the Nile."[200] He conjectured that the famed Egyptian Sphinx was in fact a monument erected by Queen Moo in memory of her deceased husband, Prince Coh.[201]

IN THE MID-1920S, just as Stacy-Judd was formulating his view that the architecture of the Maya should serve as a source for a new American architecture, there came a brief spate of renewed interest in the Atlantis theory. The impetus for all of this interest were a series of publications by the English author, Lewis Spence. Spence, who was intrigued by world-wide myths, had already written a number of books on the pre-Columbian civilizations of Meso-America and Peru.[202] In 1924, Spence published his *The Problem of Atlantis.* This was followed by *Atlantis in America* (1925) and *The History of Atlantis* (1926).[203]

SPENCE'S ARGUMENTS THAT ATLANTIS INDEED EXISTED and that the Maya represent the "carriers" of the highly developed culture of the inhabitants of the Lost continent of Atlantis obviously reinforced Stacy-Judd's belief in the primacy of Maya culture in the New World. In fact, almost all of the essential arguments advanced by Stacy-Judd for the existence of Atlantis and for the Maya being the chief remnant of that civilization were taken from Spence's writings.

STACY-JUDD INCLUDED NUMEROUS QUOTES FROM Spence's writings in his *Atlantis—Mother of Empires* along with those of Le Plongeon and others. The writings of these Atlantis apologists were almost in every case presented as irrefutable "authorities" who could be fully relied upon. But Stacy-Judd went one step further, especially with Spence. He borrowed and paraphrased him so closely at times that one often feels that one is reading Spence not Stacy-Judd.

IN HIS 1939 ATLANTIS, Stacy-Judd abandoned certain of his bizarre earlier views. He no longer advanced the notion that the earliest Egyptians were Maya colonist, though he still clung to the belief that Christ was a master of the Maya tongue and that Christ's final words were pure Maya.[204] His position in 1939 was as he states it, "In tracing the Mayas back to prehistoric times, I shall endeavor to show their profound influence upon all the great civilizations; but I do not infer that all culture, science and art originate with the Mayas. It is my belief, however, that they began the great cycle of civilizations."[205]

MARTIN RIDGE, THE BIOGRAPHER OF IGNATIUS DONNELLY, characterized the latter's approach, "Since Atlantis was basically a lawyer's brief in behalf of a speculative theory, Donnelly conformed to legal rather than scientific rules of evidence."[206] Stacy-Judd followed suit, and like Donnelly he selected the evidence which substantiated his case and discarded the rest. At the time that Stacy-Judd published his quarto sized 336 page volume, there was more than enough clear archaeological evidence attesting to the indigenous development of the Maya culture in the highlands of Guatemala and Mexico. The extensive research in this area which has been going on since 1945 has essentially solidified the case for independent origin and development.

ALTHOUGH STACY-JUDD MENTIONS the principal respected figures in Maya archaeology (he had after all met them in Yucatan or in the United States) Herbert J. Spinden, Frans Blom, Sylvanus Griswold Morley, and J. Eric Thompson, he dismisses their unanimously held view that the Maya developed their civilization independently. He banished these authorities by asserting that "There are many reputable students who do not agree with the Atlantis hypothesis; yet in recent years thousands of thinking persons are becoming enthusiastic supporters, in the face of the fact that the essentially materialistic majority always experience difficulty in accepting even the most convincing circumstantial evidence."[207]

HOW SIMILAR WAS HIS VIEW OF PROFESSIONAL archaeologists to that held by Le Plongeon? "I have been accused of promulgating notions on ancient America contrary to the opinion of men regarded as authorities. And so it is, indeed . . . But who are those pretended authorities? Certainly not the doctors and professors at the head of the universities and colleges of the United States; for not only do they know absolutely nothing of American civilization, but, judging from letters in my possession, the majority of them refuse to learn anything concerning it."[208]

OBVIOUSLY IN STACY-JUDD'S VIEW, these professional archaeologists were not thinking individuals, they were materialistic (whatever that might mean in this context), and they refused to look objectively at the overwhelming evidence of Atlantis as the source for Meso-American civilization. Stacy-Judd's premise was that "It has always appeared to me that some center other than the present designated Maya area must have existed; a center in which their civilization originated and developed to maturity."[209]

BEFORE HE COULD COMMENCE with his restructuring of the history of mankind and specially the question of the origins of Meso-American civilizations, he had to discard another contender as a source. This was the lost continent of Mu, which had supposedly been located in the Pacific Ocean. The myth of the Lost Continent of Mu was, in the thirties, even more popular and discussed than the existence of Atlantis. The chief advocate for the existence of this Pacific ocean civilization was James Churchward. This author's two books, *The Lost Continent of Mu* (1926 and 1933), and his *Children of Mu* (1931 and 1933), were a subject of amused popular discussion during the late twenties and the early thirties.[210] Churchward's contention was that not only did the "children of Mu" populate the New World (and specifically established the basis for Maya civilization), but they also populated Atlantis. "I do not wish to discredit the work of this author," Stacy-Judd wrote, "but his argument for that continent as birthplace of Mayan culture is in my opinion not tenable."[211]

THOUGH STACY-JUDD'S FOCUS WAS ON the question of the origin of the Maya (Atlantis, of course), the arrangement of his arguments for the existence and primacy of Atlantis is modeled after that of Donnelly who was highly selective of the evidence presented in his text and the accompanying illustrations. Both authors quote freely from others, generally mentioning the author of the quote, but seldom the publication itself. Their mutual assumption seems to have been that any intelligent person was aware of the authors they mention (this being, of course, an excellent PR device to suggest erudition upon the part of the authors). Stacy-Judd's quotations are more difficult to search out (for the context of the quote) than Donnelly's, since he did not indicate even the page number. Neither Donnelly's 1882 volume nor Stacy-Judd's 1939 publication incorporated a bibliography.

IT IS QUITE EVIDENT THAT THE ATLANTIS THEME was popular one in the thirties. Mable Dodge Luhan wrote him from New York that "For years I have been the sole one, who among people I see, has been asserting that the people of the east and west had a common origin in the lost continent . . . to find all this corroboration is wonderful."[212] Dr. Karl Menninger of the Menninger Clinic at Topeka, Kansas, wrote to Stacy-Judd that "Last evening a friend of mine, Mrs. Mabel Dodge Luhan, sent to my apartment [in New York] a magnificent book dealing with two things in which I have long been interested, the Mayan culture and the Atlantis theory. I enjoyed your book very much, and was only sorry that I was obliged to return it to its owner at the end of the evening."[213]

STACY-JUDD FOLLOWED THE PUBLICATION of his Atlantis volume by an illustrated article, in the February 4, 1940 *Los Angeles Times Magazine,* "Going Back to Atlantis," and by another book, *A Mayan Manuscript: Codex Merida,* published by his friends at the Philosophical Research Society.[214] A Mayan Manuscript (Codex Merida) was a manuscript recently discovered within a walled enclosure of the Cathedral of Merida. "In these rooms scores of ancient manuscripts, including the subject of this work, were discovered."[215] Photographs of the pages of this manuscript had been obtained by Theodore Willard and placed in Stacy Judd's hands for publication. Stacy-Judd reproduced the original illustrations of the manuscript and accompanied them with a partial translation.

A S AN ASIDE DURING THE LATE 1930s, Stacy-Judd designed and patented the "Hul-Che Atlatl Throwing Stick" and sold the patent to a Michigan manufacturer. This device was supposedly modeled after a Maya throwing stick.

World War II and Post-War Years

WITH THE ENTRY OF THE UNITED STATES into the Second World War in December 1941, Stacy-Judd became a Designing Engineer at the Hughes Aircraft Company in Los Angeles (1942-45). He was involved with the design of Howard Hughes' famed HK.I, the "Flying Goose" [now known as the "Spruce Goose"]. In a way it was fitting for him to be involved with Howard Hughes in this extravagant project to produce the world's largest aircraft. Whether his contribution to this project went beyond engineering and drafting remains, at this moment, unknown.

IMMEDIATELY AFTER LEAVING HUGHES he continued his efforts to design theme villages. In his "Enchanted Boundary," resort project (1944-45) near Los Angeles, he adapted many of the groups of buildings he had designed in 1938 for the "Streets of All Nations" Project. In addition to enriching the number of Maya-styled buildings, he added a few new exotic themes, including a Tibetan style building that visually dominated the village. In the middle of the vast parking lot he anticipated the later flying capsule theme building of the Los Angeles Airport, only Stacy-Judd's restaurant building was suspended on an octagonal shaft and was square, not round.

IN THE WOODED PINES OF LAKE GREGORY, CALIFORNIA, he created an "English Village" (1944) composed of one and two story half-timber buildings. As with his thirties village and resort schemes, neither the "Enchanted Boundary" resort, nor the Lake Gregory "English Village" were built. Nevertheless, he received a modest number of commissions during the years 1945-1960 for single family houses and apartment buildings, most of which were built in the San Fernando Valley where he had established his combined office and home. As with his pre-1942 houses, these dwellings play with a mildly modernist image combined with the classic California ranch house forms. None are memorable, most are competent but on the dull side. He also designed a few commercial buildings and public structures. Among his commercial ventures were the Glen Rishes drive-in restaurant in Los Angeles (1959), a hotel (unbuilt) for Guatemala City (1951), and the Morris Plan Company of California Bank building (1948-49) in Long Beach. All of these projects were non-assertive structures, and their image was lightly modern.

NEEDLESS TO SAY, STACY-JUDD had not in any way abandoned his ideal of creating an "All-American" architecture based upon that of the Maya. He republished his *The Ancient Maya* in 1951 under a new title *Kabah*. He was asked in 1951 to provide a new campus for Chapman College of the Christian University in North Hollywood. In his design for this college, in its entrance gate and the administration building, he avoided any open use of Maya ornament, and instead thought in terms of the traditional massing of Maya

Chapter 14

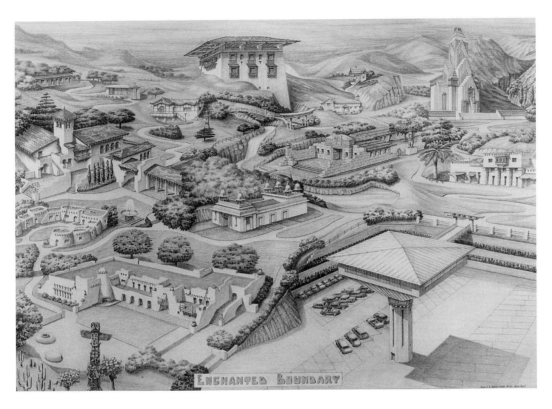

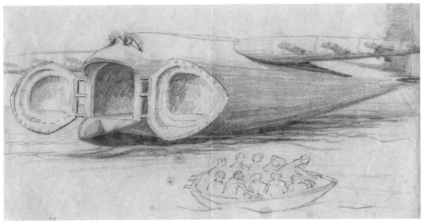

*Above: Enchanted Boundry, 1945-55,
Los Angeles; (project).
Below: Cartoon drawing by Robert B.
Stacy-Judd of Howard Hughes's "The
Flying Goose," 1942.*

Above: The English Village, 1944, Lake Gregory; (project).
Below: Prefabricated house "The American Cottage," 1948, Glendale; (project).

buildings. In his use of rows of vertical pilasters and the central high section of the administration building, he carried on into the fifties the earlier simplified versions of the Art Deco (as many other architect were also doing during these years). Though not built, his designs for Chapman College represent one of the high points of his design career. ANOTHER MAYA-INSPIRED DESIGN of these years, which was built, was the (Masonic) North Hollywood Temple Association building (1946–51) in Van Nuys.[217] In this instance, at the request of his client,

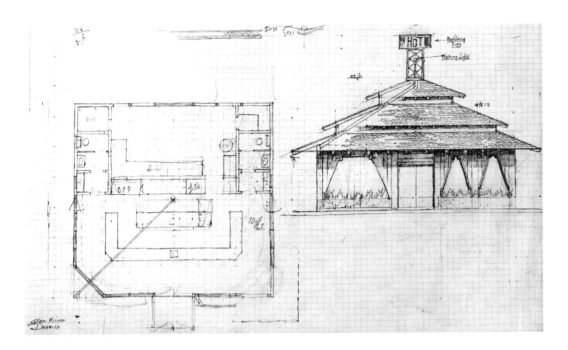

Above: Glenn Rishes Drive-in Restaurant, 1959, San Fernando Valley; (project).
Below: Chapman College, Christian University, proposed Entrance Gate, 1951, North Hollywood; (project).

he returned to an out and out Maya theme, including a sparse use of ornament. The design of this building, mixing Maya with Art Deco, Moderne, and Expressionism is similar to a number of his buildings of the 1930s.

IF IT HAD BEEN CARRIED OUT, Stacy-Judd's set designs for the projected film *The Scarlet Empress* (1949) would, perhaps, have been the culmination of his advocacy of the Maya revival. He not only designed the stage sets, but also the costumes, and even made suggestions as to the how the script could be more authentic. His advocacy of things Maya continued through his many writings published by the Philosophical Research Society. In 1951, he was interviewed on the radio (Station KFAC in Los Angeles) by the actor Guy Bates Post. Post later produced a program "Death of a Butterfly" based on parts of Stacy-Judd's The Ancient Maya. This radio experience was followed in 1953, by an interview with Edward R. Morrow over a national network.

IN THE 1950s, he patented his "Arrowlock" reinforced, interlocking concrete wall.

IT WAS IN 1949 THAT HE MARRIED AGAIN, this time to the artist and writer, Marjorie Webster. He continued to hold parties and show films at his studio home in the San Fernando Valley. In 1953, repre-

Stage Sets for the film: The Scarlet Empress, *1949.*
Above: The Encounter in the Ball Court. Below: Arrival in Chichen-Itza.

Stage Set for the film The Scarlet Empress, *1949. Left: The Sacred Fire Dance.*

senting the architects of the Valley, he was the promoter/director of the "Architect's Home Show," presented in the Armory at Burbank, California. Though the number of his commissions slowed down considerably in the later 1950s, he continued his practice up to the mid– 1960s. His largest house of these years was the Morris Brown house in Stone Canyon, Sherman Oaks (1954). Another of his commissions of the fifties was the Hesby Street School (with W. Harry Hillier) in Encino (1952-53).

IN THE LATE SIXTIES HE RETIRED from practice. In 1973 his *Atlantis Mother of Empires* was republished. He died in Canoga Park on Monday, February 10, 1975 at the age of ninety.

Asequradora-El Quetzal Hotel, 1951, Guatemala City, Mexico.
Above: Proposed building; Below: Proposed interior, The Fountain Court; (project).

*Above: Institute of Religious Science
Church, 1957, Palm Springs; (project).
Below: Church for Harold Shields, 1961,
Monterey; (project).*

Oakwood Cemetery, 1924, Chatsworth; (project).

POSTSCRIPT

IN RECENT YEARS, there has been renewed interest in the architecture of Robert E. Stacy-Judd, primarily because of its perceived wildness and exoticism. Even in these days of postmodernism and deconstructivism, no one could really take serious his argument for an "All-American Architecture," inspired by the architecture of the Maya and other Native American cultures of Meso-America. Equally, the myth of Atlantis hardly enjoys much acceptance these days.

WHAT THEN CAN BE MADE OF this maverick Englishman, who throughout his entire career flamboyantly combined a wonderful and free hucksterism, a literary career, and the practice of architecture? Though Stacy-Judd was a huckster, there is no question that he strongly believed whatever at the moment he happened to be enthusiastic about. His adventurous life as well as his sallies into the extravagant and exotic were certainly a reflection of his creative and restless personality. One can never conceive of him as simply a staid and sensible practitioner of architecture. He always seemed to be on the lookout for ideas and design approaches which lay outside of the norm. As with his advocacy of an American architecture based upon the Maya, or his involvement with the Atlantis myth, he often seized upon ideas at just the right moment. He propelled himself into national and even international attention with his Aztec Hotel. As we have seen he was by no means the first to suggest that pre-Columbian architecture could serve as a source for a new modern architecture of the twentieth century, yet the timing of this commission and his highly successful salesmanship of it transported him into the forefront of American culture.

CONSIDERING HIS CAREFUL TRAINING in architecture one would suppose that his designs would end up being sophisticated products. They are not. One has a secret suspicion that he purposely twisted each of designs out of the world of the respectable and ordinary. His buildings end up being as wild as many of the ideas he came to advocate. Respectable architects of the time felt decidedly uneasy with his designs, not only when he used exotic images, but even when he employed acceptable traditional images. His mode of attracting attention to himself was then through his off beat designs, equally matched by his aggressively outlandish (but wonderful) marketing of his ideas and personage.

AS WE HAVE SEEN, his English compatriot, Alfred Bossom, had also been to Yucatan and had suggested that Maya architecture could serve as a basis for a new American architecture, but it would be impossible to conceive of Bossom illustrated in magazine and newspaper articles as an explorer of the jungles with pith helmet and all. Perhaps, what attracts us to Stacy-Judd and to what he did is the extravagant way that he went about all of his activities, whether in architecture or in his writings. As in part a comment on ourselves, we generally find it difficult to take his designs or his ideas seriously, but at the same time we come away from them with a strong sense of exuberant delight, a quality which regrettably is missing from the contemporary world of architectural ideology and buildings.

ACKNOWLEDGMENTS

IN THE EARLY 1970S, ROBERT B. STACY-JUDD, with the encouragement of his close friends Charles and Mildred Podmore, presented his architectural and literary records to the Architectural Drawing Collection, University Art Museum, University of California. Later the Podmores presented additional materials including a number of the impressive motion picture films which Stacy-Judd had made in Yucatan and elsewhere. This collection, and the help and encouragement of the Podmores, have made this book possible.

I WOULD ALSO LIKE TO THANK MARJORIE WEBSTER (Mrs. Robert B. Stacy-Judd) and her mother Edna Robb Webster (through her letters), for their critical help and for information about Stacy-Judd. Also, Doris Bellingham, the niece of Stacy-Judd has been most helpful in clearing up a number of "mysteries" of his early family life in England. Finally, my thanks goes to Elizabeth Mjelde, who organized the Stacy-Judd archives, and compiled the initial list of buildings and projects, as well as the first draft of the bibliography. Pamela Post, assistant curator of the Architectural Drawing Collection, has, as always, contributed substantially to all aspects of this project.

— *David Gebhard*

I WISH TO THANK THE FOLLOWING FRIENDS, whose interest and enthusiasm in Robert Stacy-Judd helped make it possible to photograph the buildings shown in this book: Marjorie Webster, Myra Davis, Barbara Ling, Martha Mitchell, Robert DeBrask, Steve Behen with *Eastman Kodak Co.*, Ken Warfield, and James Wright.

—*Anthony Peres*

CHAPTER 1

1 Will C. Davis, "The Aztec Hotel," Los Angeles Evening Express (May 14, 1925):1

2 "Reviving Mayan Architecture," The New York Times (January 30, 1927): Sec. 2: 8. This editorial was based upon an article by Edgar Lloyd Hampton, "Rebirth of Prehistoric American Art," published in Current History 25 (February 1927): 624–634. The date of 1924 for the opening for the Aztec Hotel is incorrect, for the construction of the building commenced in early November 1924, and it was not completed until the late fall of 1925. See Southwest Builder and Contractor (November 7, 1924): 63. Also as a matter of fact the Aztec Hotel was not the first building designed in the United States to be inspired by pre-Columbian architecture of Mexico and Central America.

3 "Reviving Mayan Architecture," Sec. 2: 8.

4 "Ancient Mayan Motifs in New Architecture," The Christian Science Monitor (May 9, 1927): 6; "American Architecture First," Los Angeles Times (April 14, 1927) Sec. 4: 1 & 2.

5 Ibid.

6 "Hollywood Architect to Explore Mysteries of Mayan Pyramid," Los Angeles Herald Examiner (January 11, 1933): 3.

7 "Robert Stacy-Judd, A Hughes Notable," Hughesnews 5\16 (August 18, 1944): 3.

CHAPTER 2

8 Robert B. Stacy-Judd, The Autobiography of An Architect. (Unpublished manuscript, written in Los Angeles, c. 1944): 10.

9 Ibid., p. 1.

10 The information about Stacy-Judd's father's occupation and other facts relating to his childhood have been provided by Mrs. Doris Bellingham of Warminster, England, the daughter of his brother. Letters to the author, dated November 20, 1992, January 1, 1993, and February 18, 1993.

11 Stacy-Judd, Autobiography, p. 1.

12 Ibid.

13 Ibid., p. 20.

14 Ibid., p. 39.

15 Ibid., p. 40-41.

16 Alastair Service, Edwardian Architecture. (Oxford University Press, New York and Toronto, 1977).

17 Stacy-Judd, Autobiography, p. 44-45.

18 The drawings for this school contain the notation "Designed by R–B–S–J while a pupil of James Thompson. 1904."

19 Stacy-Judd, Autobiography, p. 72.

20 Robert B. Stacy-Judd, Stroud and His Son: Their Book (c. 1905)

21 Stacy-Judd, Autobiography, p. 108.

22 Robert W. Carden, "The Franco-British Exhibition," Architectural Record 14 (August 1908): 83- 97. The only Stacy-Judd drawings for the exposition that bear his signature are structural drawings.

23 Stacy-Judd, Autobiography, p. 136

24 According to Stacy-Judd's notes, the Short-Story Time Table was published during the years 1909 and 1910. The "Preface" by Major Gillespie-Addison implies that the November 1909 issue was the first of the time

Footnotes

tables. Only two copies are present in the Stacy-Judd collection in the Architectural Drawing Collection, University Art Museum, University of California Santa Barbara. These are for the months of November 1909 and March 1910. These small red booklets were published by Robert B. Stacy-Judd and his partner William P. Wells. The short story in the November issue is "Carden Reece,;" that in the March 1910 issue, "On the Threshold of Death."

25 Stacy-Judd, Autobiography, p. 146.

26 Robert B. Stacy-Judd, Gems from Ye Magic Toy Cave, R. Prentice, His Notes (1909)

27 Stacy-Judd, Autobiography, p. 148. The Stacy- Judd Collection within the Architectural Drawing Collection, University Art Museum University of California does not contain any documentation relating to the Prentice Building. He only states in his autobiography that it was built.

28 Ibid., p. 149.

29 Ibid., p. 152.

30 Ibid., p. 174.

31 Ibid., p. 166.

CHAPTER 3

32 Stacy-Judd, Autobiography, p. 215.

33 Ibid., p. 132.

34 Ibid., p. 235-236.

35 Ibid., p. 242.

36 Ibid., p. 242. For a general picture of North Dakota architecture see: Ronald L. M. Ramsey, In the Architect's Eye: 100 Years of North Dakota Building. (Moorhead: Plains Art Museum, 1989)

37 "The Trials of the Pioneer Architect," The Western Architect 26 (December 1917): 46

38 William T. Comstock, The Architects' Directory and Specification Index for 1905-06 (New York: William T. Comstock, 1905):

39, listed 17 architects in practice within North Dakota.

39 Stacy-Judd tended throughout his autobiography to use fictitious names, so that the actual name of his partner in Minot was not mentioned. The name, Ole Mason employed in his text, was a name made up by Stacy-Judd. Frost's name occurs though on the drawings for the Elks Home at Williston, North Dakota.

40 Stacy-Judd, Autobiography, p. 248.

41 While in his partnership with Frost, Stacy-Judd designed (proposed and constructed) the following buildings: Opera House, Minot (1914); Hotel Minot, Minot (1914); Williston Hotel, Williston (1914). There were also several unidentified residential designs from these first few months of 1914 in Minot.

42 Stacy-Judd, Autobiography, p. 249.

43 "Biographical Data Regarding RBS-J," as requested by George Belding, New York City Literary Agent (June, 1959), p. 2.

44 Robert B. Stacy-Judd, "'The Mint House,' Pevensey, Sussex, England," The Western Architect 24 (July, 1916): 103-105.

45 Robert B. Stacy-Judd, Tales from Old Times (Minot: privately published, 1914); Dracula (Minot: unpublished, 1914). The quote from a local newspaper is contained in "Biographical Information regarding RBS-J...," (June, 1959). In the Architectural Drawing Collection, University Art Museum, University of California, Santa Barbara.

46 Stacy-Judd, Autobiography, p. 341.

47 United States Department of Labor, Report of the United States Housing Corporation, Vol. II, Houses, Site-Planning, Utilities. (Washington: Government Printing Office, 1919).

48 Frederick Law Olmsted, Jr., "Lessons From Housing Developments of the United States Housing Corporation," Labor Statistics

Bureau Monthly Labor Review, 8 (May 1919):27-38.

CHAPTER 4

49 There were several commissions dating from 1919 undertaken after he returned to Minot (such as the Tatley-Hughes Court). Whether these commissions were pre-War hold-overs or new projects we do not know, nor can we be certain what his intent was when he returned to Minot.

50 Stacy-Judd, Autobiography, p. 356.

51 Major and Stacy-Judd, "Empire Theatre, Edmonton, Alberta, Canada," Western Architect 31 (December, 1921): pls. 13 & 14.

52 Stacy-Judd, Autobiography, p. 358.

53 There are nine of these articles from the Calgary Daily Herald in the Architectural Drawing Collection, University Art Museum, University of California, Santa Barbara.

54 Robert B. Stacy-Judd ("Buildicus"), "Chats on Practical Architecture," Calgary Daily Herald, the fourth in the series, undated and unpaged. Based on the dating of the third and fifth in the series, this article was published early in March 1922.

55 Robert B. Stacy-Judd, ("Buildicus"), "Chats on Practical Architecture," Calgary Daily Herald, undated, and unpaged (c. 1922).

56 Robert B. Stacy-Judd, ("Buildicus"), "Chats on Practical Architecture," Calgary Daily Herald, undated, unpaged (c. 1922).

57 Robert B. Stacy-Judd ("Buildicus"), "Chats on Practical Architecture," Calgary Daily Herald (March 18, 1922), no page.

CHAPTER 5

58 Stacy-Judd, Autobiography, p. 359.

59 David Gebhard, Lutah Maria Riggs: A Woman in Architecture, 1921-1980. (Santa Barbara: Capra Press, 1992): 9.

60 "The Ben Hansen House, Brentwood Heights," The Home Builder 5 (September, 1926): 11.

61 Banister Fletcher, A History of Architecture on the Comparative Method. (London: B. T. Batsford, Ltd., 1954 edition), 35, pl.B. Stacy-Judd's Library contained an earlier edition of this volume.

62 Egypt in LA. (Long Beach: The Art Galleries California State University, 1977).

CHAPTER 6

63 The Building Permit for the Aztec Hotel was listed in the Southwest Builder and Contractor 64 (November 7, 1924): 63.

64 Robert B. Stacy-Judd, "Maya or Aztec Architecture," Architect and Engineer 35 (May 1926): 55-64

65 Stacy-Judd, Autobiography, p. 348-349.

66 Victor Wolfgang von Hagen, Maya Explorer, John Lloyd Stephens and the Lost Cities of Central America. (Norman: University of Oklahoma Press, 1947). Victor Wolfgang von Hagen, Frederick Catherwood, Archt. (New York: Oxford University Press, 1950). Accompanied by Catherwood, Stephens had published other travel books on Jerusalem, Baalbec, Thebes and Karnak. Catherwood published another volumes of his Maya drawings in 1854, Incidents of Travel in Central America. (London: Hall, Virtue & Co., 1864).

67 The Hockenbury Systems, Inc. assisted the local Monrovia Community Hotel Association in organizing and obtaining the needed financing for the project. See: "Aztec Breathes of Olden Days," Pacific Coast Record 16 (October 1925): 9-10.

68 Stacy-Judd, Autobiography, p.349.

69 Ibid., p. 350.

70 Ibid., p. 351.

71 "An Adaption of Mayan Architecture," Architecture and Building 58 (June, 1926): 77.

72 The plates from the Stephen's volume which Stacy- Judd utilized for his ornamentation of the Aztec Hotel are found in volume II. They are opposite pp. 259, 309, 318, 344, 354, and 434. The interior mural decorations were derived from the various plates illustrating Maya Stele contained in volume I. To these strictly Maya motifs Stacy-Judd added a variety of geometric patterns of repeated steeped motifs, triangles, etc. which are more like Native American Southwest pottery and textile decoration than with that of the pre-Columbian art of Yucatan.

Stacy-Judd himself reproduced a number of Catherwood's plates in the printed version of a talk "Mayan Architecture—Its Adapta-bility to Modern Conditions" presented at three meetings of the Architectural League of Hollywood. These lectures were presented on July 27, August 3, and August 10, 1927.

73 Robert B. Stacy-Judd, "Maya or Aztec Architecture," Architect and Engineer 35 (May 1926): 59.

74 ."An Adaption of Mayan Architecture," Architecture and Building 58 (June 1926): 77.

75 "Maya Influence in Southern California Decoration," Good Furniture Magazine 27 (October 1926): 182.

76 "An Adaption of Mayan Architecture," Architecture and Building 58 (June 1926): 77.

77 Francis S. Onderdonk, The Ferro-Concrete Style. (New York: Architectural Book Publishing Company, 1928): 98-100.

CHAPTER 7

78 Letter from Rexford Newcomb to Stacy-Judd, dated August 24, 1927.

79 Editors, Western Architect, "Comments on a review of George Oakley Totten, Maya Architecture by Rexford Newcomb, Western Architect 36 (July 1927): 116.

80 Carleton Monroe Winslow, "The Architect's Viewpoint," Architect and Engineer 104 (March 1931): 91.

81 Herbert Howe Bancroft, Book of the Fair: An Historical and Descriptive Presentation of the World's Science, Art and Industry. 10 vols. (Chicago: Bancroft Publishing Co., 1893), vol. 3, p. 636.

82 Eugen Neuhaus, The San Diego Garden Fair. (San Francisco: Paul Elder & Company, 1916), 45-46; Edgar Lee Hewett, "Ancient America at the Panama-California Exposition," Art and Archaeology 2:3 (March 1915): 65-102; Rexford Newcomb, "The New Maya Murals at San Diego," Western Architect 33 (March 1924): 32-35; Rexford Newcomb, "Aboriginal American Architectural Types," Western Architect 36 (July 1927): 110.

83 Claude Joseph Desire Charnay, The Ancient Cities of the New World: Being Voyages and Explorations in Mexico and Central America. (New York, 1887); A P. and A. C. Maudslay, A Glimpse at Guatemala, and Some Notes on the Ancient Monuments of Central America. (London, 1899). For a recent discussion of Claude J. D. Charney see: Keith F. Davis, Desire Charnay: Expeditionary Photographer. (Albuquerque: University of New Mexico Press, 1981). See Robert L. Brunhouse, Pursuit of the Ancient Maya: Some Archaeologists of Yesterday. (Albuquerque: University of New Mexico Press, 1975).

84 "From Chichen Itza, Yucatan," American Architect and Building News 20, September 4, 1886: 113; L. Viajero, "Mitla, and Other Ancient Cities of Mexico," American Architect and Building News, 61 (September 19, 1898): 85-86, plus two plates with four illustrations. Other illustrations were published in the early years of the century in such magazines as Architecture and Building, 46 (March, 1916): 102 ("Uxmal, Palacio Del Gobernador").

85 Eugene Viollet-le-Duc, The Habitations of Man in All Ages. (translated by Benjamin Bucknall) (Boston: James R. Osgood and Company, 1876) (original edition in French, 1875): Figs. 86 and 87.

86 Auguste Choisy, Historie de L'Architecture. (two volumes), (Paris: Editions Vincent, Freal & Co., 1899): vol. 2, p.161–168.

87 Banister Fletcher, A History of Architecture on the Comparative Method. (London: B. T. Batsford Ltd., 1954) (first edition, 1896), 932–933.

88 Sylvanius G. Morley, "Excavations at Quirigua, Guatemala," National Geographic Magazine 24 (March 1913): 339–361; "The Foremost Intellectual Achievement of Ancient America: The Hieroglypic Inscriptions on the Monuments of the Ruined Cities of Mexico, Guatemala, and Honduras Are Yielding the Secrets of the Maya Civilization," National Georgraphic Magazine 41 (January 1922): 109–130; "Chichen Itza, An Ancient America Mecca," National Georgraphic Magazine 42 (January, 1925): 63–95. During the years 1910–1920 Morley also wrote other articles which were published in the Bulletin of the Pan American Union and Scientific American.

89 Herbert J. Spinden, "Creating a National Art," Natural History 19 (June 1919): 622–630.

90 Thomas A. Joyce, Mexican Archaeology. (New York and London: Philip Lee Warner, 1914) (New York: Kraus Reprint Co., 1969); Sylvanus G. Morley, An Introduction to the Study of Maya Hieroglyphs. (Washington, D.C.: Bureau of American Ethnology, Bulletin 57, 1915); Herbert J. Spinden, Ancient Civilizations of Mexico and Central America. (New York: American Museum of Natural History, Handbook Series, No. 3, 1917); Herbert J. Spinden, A Study of Maya Art, Its Subject Matter and Historical Development.

(Cambridge: The Peabody Museum of Harvard University, Memoirs 6, 1913); 1–285.

CHAPTER 8

91 Marjorie Ingle, Mayan Revival Style. (Salt Lake City: Peregrine Smith Books, 1984).

92 George Oakley Totten, Maya Architecture. (Washington, D.C.: The Maya Press, 1926, and reissued in 1928).

93 Sylvanus G. Morley, "Unearthing America's Ancient History," National Georgraphic Magazine 60 (January 1931): 99–126; "Yucatan, Home of the Gifted Maya," National Geographic Magazine 70 (May 1936): 590– 644.

94 Earl H. Morris, The Temple of the Warriors at Chichen Itza. (New York: Charles Scribner's Sons, 1931). Edward T. Hinderliter, "The Maya Temple of the 1933 Chicago World's Fair," (an abstract of a paper presented at the 24th Annual Meeting of the Society of Architectural Historians, Chicago, January 28–31, 1971). Journal of the Society of Architectural Historians 30 (October, 1971): 239–240.

95 Titiana Proskouriakoff, An Album of Maya Architecture. (Washington D.C.: Carnegie Institute of Washington, 1946) Publication 558.

96 Sylanus Griswold Morley, The Ancient Maya. (Stanford: Stanford University Press, 1946 and 1947); J. Eric S. Thompson, The Rise and Fall of Maya Civilization. (Norman: University of Oklahoma Press, 1954).

97 "A Study in Moulded Granite Facing for Buildings," Southwest Contractor and Manufacture 11 (May 17, 1913): 8.

98 Alfred C. Bossom, "New Styles in American Architecture," Worlds Work (June 1926): 189.

99 Herbert F. Angel, "Pre-Columbian Architecture Comes Back," Pan American Magazine 43 (August 1930): 91–107.

100 Edgar Lloyd Hampton, "American Architecture First," Los Angeles Times, (April 24, 1927): Feature: 2.

101 Robert B. Stacy-Judd, "An Appeal to the Young Architect," notes for an Architectural Exhibition at the Building Center, Los Angeles, April 15 to May 15, 1964. Stacy-Judd Collection, ADC.

102 Stacy-Judd, Autobiography, Figs. 84-87.

103 "Aztec House," American Architect and Building News 29 (July 5, 1890): 13.

104 The first mention of the historical significance of this building within the pre-Columbian revival was contained in David Gebhard and Robert Winter, A Guide to Architecture in Los Angeles and Southern California. (Salt Lake City: Peregrine Smith Books, 1977): 208.

105 Advertisement of the Atlas Portland Cement Co., Architect and Engineer 32 (March 1913): 34.

106 Across the street from the Cordova Hotel was a second apartment hotel, designed by the same architectural firm. This was the 1912 Abbey Hotel. While the facade of the Abbey Hotel was Gothic, the architects injected Pre-Columbian face masks into the wide lintel above the first floor pilasters.

107 C. Matlack Price, "The Pan American Union Building and its Annex: Washington D.C.," Architectural Record 34 (November 1913): 384-457. The Aztec fountain in the patio was designed by Mrs. H. P. Whitney (Gertrude Vanderbilt), and the pre-Columbian tile work was by J. H. Dulles Allen.

108 George Oakley Totten, Maya Architecture. (Washington, D.C.: The Maya Press, 1926); 238. What is left unclear is whether Albert Kelsey's visits to Yucatan preceded or came after the completion of the Pan American Union building.

109 Ibid., p. 447.

110 Southwest Museum Subway Opens," Los Angeles Times (March 7, 1920): Sec. 5: 5.

111 It should be noted that these Maya details are not revealed in the existing partial set of Gill's working drawings for the Clark house. These features, plus the projecting vegas, could well have been added by the Clark's.

112 An illustration of Totten's design for the proposed museum is to be found in the article by Herbert E. Angel, "Pre-Columbian Architecture Comes Back," Pan American Magazine 43 (August 1930): 92.

113 "To Design a Museum Building to Lodge Indian Americana," American Architect 116, (July 9, 1919): 49.

114 Ibid.: 49.

115 George Oakley Totten, Maya Architecture. (Washington D.C.: The Maya Press, 1926).

CHAPTER 9

116 Dennis Sharp, Alfred C. Bossom's American Architecture, 1903-1926. (London: Book Art, 1984).

117 Alfred C. Bossom published one of the widely used books in the twenties on Mexican architecture. This was his An Architectural Pilgrimage in Old Mexico. (New York: Charles Scribner's, 1924). For his activities at Tikal see: "Restoration of the Ancient City of Tikal, Guatemala," American Architect 129 (January 20, 1926): 266.

118 Alfred C. Bossom, Building to the Skies: The Romance of the Skyscraper. (New York and London: The Studio, Ltd., 1934); 48.

119 "Color Dominant in Design of the Union Trust Building, Detroit, Michigan" (designed by Smith, Hinchman and Grylls), American Architect 136 (November 1929): 32-39.

120 "The Marine Building, Vancouver, B.C.," Architect and Engineer 104 (January

1931): 60-62; William I. Garren, "The Berkeley Public Library," Architect and Engineer 104 (January 1931): 26-36.

121 B. J. S. Cahill, "Four-Fifty Sutter Street," Architect and Engineer 101 (April, 1930): 35- 52. William I. Garren," Civilization: Metal and Architects," Architect and Engineer 100 (February 1930): 42-48; B. J. S. Cahill, "Four-Fifty Sutter Street," Architect and Engineer 101 (April, 1930): 35- 52.

122 "Notable Advance Shown in Development of Junior High School Schools of Los Angeles," Southwest Builder and Contractor (September 6, 1929): 38-40.

123 Carleton Monroe Winslow, "The Architect's Viewpoint," Architect and Engineer 104 (March 1931): 91.

124 "The Fisher Theater, Graven and Mayger, architects," American Architect 135 (February 20, 1929): 269-276; Francisco Cornejo, "Description of Architecture and Decorations of the Mayan Theater," Pacific Coast Architect (April 1928): 13-30; Donald E. Marquis, "Archaeological Aspects of the Mayan Theater of Los Angeles," Art and Archaeology (March 1930): 99- 111, 124.

125 Roberta Deering and Joseph McElroy, The Historic Structures of Stolp Island. (Aurora: City of Aurora, 1985),26-27.

126 The Hotel President in Kansas City was built in 1926, and was design by the firm of Clarence E. Shepard and Albert C. Wiser. See: "Hotel President," Western Architect 36 (July, 1927): Pls. 122-125. Maya Room Madrillon Restaurant, Washington, D.C., illustrated in Herbert E. Angel, "Pre-Columbian Architecture Comes Back," Pan American Magazine 43 (August 1930): 97.

127 Elbert S. Somers, "Mayan Architecture and Its Adaptation," Architect and Engineer 104 (February, 1931): 61-68. Somers received his California license to practice architecture in 1921; beyond this, little is know about his work in California.

128 In his 1923 publication Batchelder Tile Catalogue of Hand Made Tiles (Los Angeles) Ernest Batchelder illustrated on page 30 nineteen of his Maya tiles, and on page 33 he illustrated a Maya Console. We do not know what month in 1923 the catalogue was published, but it would seem likely that these Maya tiles were produced as early as 1922. Examples of "Aztec Tile" produced by the California Clay Products Co. see: Pacific Coast Architect, 26 (July 1924): back cover advertisement; Southwest Builder and Contractor (September 16, 1927): 29. Catalogue of Malibu Potteries. (Reproduction of the original catalogue of Malibu Potteries, by the Malibu Lagoon Museum, 1990); 18 and 20. Tiles, fireplace surrounds, etc. employing Pre-Columbian motifs were produced by many tile manufacturers in Southern California, including Tropico Potteries (owned from 1922 on by Gladding, McBean and Company), and Pomona Tile Co.

129 An example in Griffin's work would be his "Solid Rock House," 1911, Winnetka. See David T. Van Zanten, Walter Burley Griffin: Selected Designs. (Palos Park: Prairie School Press, 1970), 33. Several Wright examples would be the entrance loggia to his Oak Park Studio, 1895; Unity Temple, 1906, Oak Park, and the Midway Gardens, 1914, Chicago. See Henry-Russell Hitchcock, In the Nature of Materials: 1887-1941, The Buildings of Frank Lloyd Wrigh(New York: Duell, Sloane and Pearce, 1942), figs. 38. 118, 193.

130 Hitchcock, In the Nature, figs. 202 and 204. The first full critical treatment of Wright's use of the Pre-Columbian is contained in Dimitri Tselos, "Exotic Influences in the Architecture of Frank Lloyd Wright," Magazine of Art 47 (April 1953): 160-169, 184.

131 Donald Hoffman, Frank Lloyd Wright's Hollyhock House. (New York: Dover Publications, Inc., 1992); Kathryn Smith, Frank Lloyd Wright: Hollyhock House and Olive Hill: Buildings and Projects for Aline Barnsdall. (New York: Rizzoli, 1992). For illustration of Wright's California buildings see: David Gebhard, Romanza: The California Architecture of Frank Lloyd Wright. (San Francisco: Chronicle Books, 1988).

132 David Gebhard and Harriette Von Breton, Lloyd Wright Architect. (Santa Barbara: Art Galleries, University of California, 1971); 33.

133 Ibid., p. 47.

CHAPTER 10

134 Stacy-Judd produced two designs for the motel/hotel at Beaumont. The first was based on Maya motifs, the second design utilized a Spanish Colonial Revival image.

135 La Jolla Beach and Yacht Club, La Jolla California. (Chula Vista: Denrich Press, c. 1926) (designed by and text by Robert B. Stacy-Judd); Horace T. Major, "Why San Diego Needs Community Advertising," San Diego Business (September 1, 1926): 16-23.

136 Major, "Why San Diego," p. 23.

137 Text accompanying a prespective drawing for the Carey house, written by Stacy-Judd.

138 The Worrell house and the Sission house were both published in the upper-middle-class home shelter magazine, Arts and Decoration. Mary Barbara Dennis, "A Modern House with Indian Atmosphere," Arts and Decoration 28 (November, 1927): 76 and 108; "Norman English Design for Los Angeles Home of Charm," Arts and Decoration 28 (April, 1928): 75.

139 Robert B. Stacy-Judd, "Beverlyridge," California Home Owner 3 (May 1925): 20-21, 30.

140 Joe Minister, "Soboba Indian Village," Pacific Coast Record 18 (July 1927): 6.

141 Edgar Lloyd Hampton, "In Aboriginal Homes We Now Can Live," New York Times Magazine (October 30, 1927): 21.

142 Joe Minster, "Soboba Indian Village," p. 8.

143 Robert B. Stacy-Judd, "Some Local Examples of Mayan Adaptations," Architect and Engineer 30 (February 1934): 29.

144 "Mayan Architecture, Evolved from Huts, Adapted for Modern Mansion," Herald Express (March 26, 1934): Sec. B, 1.

145 "Mayan Architecture in Beverly," The Beverly Hills Citizen (November 21, 1929): 1.

146 Robert B. Stacy-Judd, "Wanted an All-American Architecture," Architect and Engineer 115 (Oct. 1933): 17.

147 David G. DeLong, Bruce Goff: Towards Absolute Architecture. (Cambridge: M.I.T. Press, 1988) (the Boston Avenue Methodist Church, 1926), 31. Sally Kitt Chappell and Ann Van Zanten, Barry Byrne, John Lloyd Wright: Architecture and Design. (Chicago: Chicago Historical Society, 1982) (Project for Church of Christ the King, Cork, Ireland, 1929), 25.

148 Stacy-Judd, Autobiography, p. 377.

149 Ibid., p. 379.

150 Robert B. Stacy-Judd, The Architect's Cost and Profit. (Hollywood: Architectural League of Hollywood, c.1926).

151 Robert B. Stacy-Judd, Mayan Architecture—Its Adaptability to Modern Conditions. (Los Angeles: Southwest Builder and Contractor, c. 1927).

152 "Personal amd Trade Notes," Southwest Builder and Contractor (August 13, 1926): 43.

153 Robert B. Stacy-Judd, "The Santa Barbara Earthquake: A True Story," This unpublished article on his experience in the Santa Barbara earthquake was written for publication. It is undated, but was probably written within a few days after he returned to his home and office in Hollywood.

154 Ibid.

155 "Construction lessons by Santa Barbara Quake Reviewed by Los Angeles Architect," Southwest Builder and Contractor (August 28, 1925): 43-44.

CHAPTER 11

156 Rupert Hughes, The War of the Maya Kings. (Philadelphia: Winston, 1952). Edna Robb Webster, Early Exploring in Lands of the Maya. (Sherman Oaks: Wilmar Publishers, 1973).

157 Theodore Arthur Willard, (1862-1943; see obituary New York Times, (February 4, 1943): 23; The City of the Sacred Well. (London: W. Heinemann, 1926); The Wizard of Zacna. (Boston: The Stratford Company, 1929); The Bride of the Rain God: Princess of Chichen Itza. (Cleveland: The Burrow Brothers Co., 1930); Kukulcan, The Bearded Conqueror. (Hollywood: Murray and Gee, 1931); The Lost Empires of the Itzaes and Mayas. (Glendale: Arthur Clark Company, 1933).

158 Letter of Stacy Judd to Edna Robb Webster, dated October 28, 1929.

159 Stacy-Judd, Letter to Edna Robb Webster, dated January 16, 1930.

160 Edna Robb Webster, "Mystery of the Loltun Cave Hermit." A copy of this newspaper article, sent out by Everyweek Magazine, NEA Service, Inc., Cleveland, Ohio, is contained in the Stacy-Judd Collection, Architectural Drawing Collection, Univ. Art Museum, Univ. of California, Santa Barbara.

161 Robert B. Stacy-Judd, Telegram to The NEA Service Ind., Cleveland, Ohio, dated December 29, 1930.

162 Robert B. Stacy-Judd, Letter to Edna Robb Webster, dated January 2, 1931.

163 "Motion Pictures Taken in Exploring Ancient Maya Ruins in Yucatan," Southwest Builder and Contractor, (September 5, 1930): 35.

164 The Ancient Maya was also published in 1934, by Murray and Gee, Los Angeles. In 1951, Stacy-Judd republished the book, making no changes, but providing a new title, Kabah. (Hollywood: House-Warven, 1951).

165 Front dusk jacket from Kabah. (Hollywood: House-Warven, 1951).

166 Robert B. Stacy-Judd, "Wanted: An All- American Architecture with Ancient Mayan Motifs as a Background," Part 1, Architect and Engineer 115 (October 1933): 10-19; "Mayan Art and the Classics," Part II, Architect and Engineer 115 (November 1933): 33-40; "An All-American Architecture," Part III, Architect and Engineer 115 (December, 1933): 29-36; "An All-American Architecture, Part IV, Architect and Engineer 116 (January 1934): 29-38; "Some Local Examples of Mayan Adaptations," Part V, Architect and Engineer 116 (February 1934): 21-30.

167 "Announcing a Series of Articles on Mayan Architecture," Architect and Engineer 114 (September, 1933): 41-42. In a letter written to William James in Pullman, Washington, on September 18, 1936, he was still thinking of publishing this projected book. "The Architect and Engineer, published in San Francisco (Foxcroft Bldg.) ran a series of five articles of mine entitled "Wanted, An All-American Architecture." . . . I hope shortly to enlarge this series and make them of book length." Letter in the Stacy-Judd Collection, ADC, University Art Museum, University of California, Santa Barbara.

168 "Notes and Comments," Architect and Engineer, 122 (August, 1935): 7.

169 Ibid, p. 41; Gerhardt T. Krammer, "Maya Design," Architect and Engineer 122 (September 1935): 21-35, 41.

170 Ibid., p. 21.

171 Ibid., p. 25.

172 Stacy-Judd, "Maya Architecture: Architect- Explorer Replies to Critic," Architect and Engineer, 124 (February 1936): 19-23.

173 Ibid., p. 20.

174 Ibid., p. 22.

175 Ibid., p. 22.

176 Ibid., p. 23.

177 Robert B. Stacy-Judd, Autobiography. (Third copy), (Los Angeles: unpublished, c. 1965): Chapter 37: 2.

178 Robert L. Brunhouse, Frans Blom, Maya Explorer. (Albuquerque: University of New Mexico Press, 1976): 119.

179 Stacy-Judd, Autobiography, Chapter 37, 8.

180 Stacy-Judd mentioned in his "Outline of RBS-J Activities as Requested by Gordon Belding, Literary Agent, in Re MS 'Personal Pronoun,' June 1959," that he visited Guatemala in 1951, He noted, "At ruins and Antigua." It would appear from his various notes that he may have visited Guatemala earlier, sometime in the late 1930s.

CHAPTER 12

181 Robert B. Stacy-Judd, "Some Local Examples of Mayan Adaptation," Architect and Engineer 116 (February 1934): 29.

182 Ibid.,p. 28.

183 Ibid., The Philosophical Research Society, The Philosophy of Purposeful Living. (Los Angeles: The Philosophical Research Society, 1945); 21.

185 Manly Palmer Hall, Atlantis, An Interpretation. (Los Angeles: The Philosophical Research Society, c.1946).

186 Manly Palmer Hall, Francis Bacon: The Concealed Poet. (Los Angeles: Philosopical Research Society, c. 1940); The Mystery of Electricity: A Retrospective and a Prophecy. (London: "The Rally," 1932).

187 Gerhardt T. Krammer, "Maya Design," Architect and Engineer, 122 (September 1935): 26-27.

188 Stacy-Judd, letter to I. Henry Harris, dated March 21, 1941; ADC, University Art Museum, University of California, Santa Barbara. Harris was one of the incorporators of the company.

189 John L. Stephens, Incidents of Travel in Central America and Yucatan. (New York: Harper & Brothers, 1841): Vol. II, 442-443.

CHAPTER 13

190 Ignatius Donnelly, Atlantis: The Antediluvian World. (New York: Harper and Brothers, 1882).

191 Martin Ridge, Ignatius Donnelly: The Portrait of a Politician. (Chicago: The University of Chicago Press, 1962).

192 Ignatius Donnelly, The Great Cryptogram. (Chicago: R. S. Peale and Co., 1887); The Cipher in the Plays, and on the Tombstone. (Minneapolis: The Verulam Publishing Company, 1899).

193 Plato, The Works of Plato. (translated by B. Jowett), (New York: Tudor Publishing Co., n.d.), Part 2,:p. 370-371.

194 Ibid.,p. 377-398.

195 Ignatius Donnelly, Atlantis: The Antediluvian World. (New York: Harper and Brothers, 1882), 348.

196 Robert L. Brunhouse, Pursuit of the Ancient Maya. (Albuquerque: University of New Mexico Press, 1975), 86, 156. William E. Gates, The Spirit of the Hour in Archaeology, Papers of the School of Antiquity, No. 1, (Point Loma, California, 1917), 16-17.

197 Donnelly, Atlantis,p. 1-2.

198 Stacy-Judd, Autobiography, p. 329.

199 Jules Verne, Twenty Thousand Leagues Under the Sea. (Paris: P. J. Hetzel, 1869), Pt. II, "A Vanished Continent."

200 Augustus Le Plongeon, Queen Moo and the Egyptian Sphinx. (New York: Published by the Author, 1900), xix. Le Plongeon had visted Yucatan and had conducted excavations of a sort there. A copy annotated by Stacy-Judd of the Le Plongeon book is in the Stacy-Judd Collection, at the Architectural Drawing Collection, University Art Museum, University of California Santa Barbara.

201 Ibid., p. xix.

202 Among these works of Lewis Spence was his The Civilization of Ancient Mexico. (New York: G. P. Putnam's, 1912).

203 Lewis Spence, Atlantis in America. (New York: Brentano's, 1925); The History of Atlantis. (London, W. Rider and Son, Ltd., 1926). A copy of Spence's Atlantis in America, with annotated notes by Stacy-Judd, is contained in the Stacy-Judd Collection, Architectural Drawing Collection, University Art Museum, University of California Santa Barbara.

204 Robert B. Stacy-Judd, Atlantis Mother of Empires. (Santa Monica: DeVorss and Company, 1939, 1973); 269-280.

205 Stacy-Judd, Atlantis: 4.

206 Ridge, Ignatius Donnelly, p. 198.

207 Stacy-Judd, Atlantis: p. 3.

208 Le Plongeon, Queen Moo, p. xxi. This passage is marked within Stacy-Judd's own copy of this book.

209 Stacy-Judd, Atlantis,p. 2.

210 James Churchward, The Los Continent of Mu. (first published in 1926), (New York: W. E. Rudge, 1933); The Children of Mu. (New York: Washburn, 1931 and 1933).

211 Stacy-Judd, Atlantis: 22-23.

212 Mabel Dodge Luhan, letter to Stacy-Judd, dated January 26, 1940. In the Architectural Drawing Collection, University Art Museum, University of California, Santa Barbara.

213 Karl Menninger, letter to Stacy-Judd, dated January 26, 1940. Architectural Drawing Collection, University Art Museum, University of California Santa Barbara.

214 Robert B. Stacy-Judd and Sam Bagby, "Going Back to Atlantis," Los Angeles Times Magazine (February 25, 1940): 7-8; Robert B. Stacy-Judd, A Maya Manuscript: Codex Merida. (Los Angeles: Philosophical Research Society, 1940).

215 Ibid.,p. 19.

CHAPTER 14

216 Stacy Judd, Kabah. (Hollywood: House-Warven, Publishers, 1951).

217 The Masonic Temple in North Hollywood was designed by Stacy-Judd, together with J. A. Murrey. See: Southwest Builder and Contractor, (March 21, 1947): 43.

1903-1912:

Metropole Hotel entrance hall, 1903
Southend-on-Sea, Sussex
(for James Thompson)

James Thompson residence, 1903
Southend-on-Sea, Sussex
(for James Thompson)

Proj.: Unidentified public building, 1904
(for James Thompson)

Proj.: Proposed Schools, 1904
Bournmouth Park, Southend-on-Sea
(for James Thompson)

Empire Hotel and Theatre, 1904-5
Birmingham
(for James Thompson)

Proj.: Masonic Temple, c. 1905
Southend-on-Sea
(for James Thompson)

Proj.: Unidentified office building, 1906-7
West End, London

Proj.: King's Cross Hotel for
Great Northern Railway Company, 1906-8
King's Cross Terminus, London, England

Franco-British Exposition, 1907-8
Shepherds Bush, London, England
(Supervising architect)

Lord Stretford de Canning residence
addition and alterations, 1908-9
Tunbridge Wells, Kent, England

Alexandra Library alterations, 1909
Eastbourne, England

Mansell's Picture Hall proscenium mural, 1910
Eastbourne, England

Proj.: Escalator, 1911,
Battery, Ventnor

Proj.: Seaside Hotel, Marylebone, London,
1911

Electric Picture Palace, 1910-12
Ventnor, Isle of Wight

Proj.: Palace Theater, 1912
Ventnor, Isle of Wight

1913-1919:

Auto show booth, 1914
Minot, North Dakota

Proj.: Emery Mapes residence, 1914
Minneapolis, Minnesota

Proj.: Opera House, 1914
Minot, North Dakota

Proj.: Unidentified residence, 1914
Minot, North Dakota

The Delfraine Project (Minot Subdivisions),
c. 1914
Minot, North Dakota

Proj.: Hotel Minot, 1914
Minot, North Dakota

Williston Hotel, c. 1914
Williston, North Dakota

Elks Home (with R.T. Frost), 1914-15
Williston, North Dakota

Union National Bank addition, 1914-15
Minot, North Dakota

Bethania Lutheran Church, 1915
Minot, North Dakota

Episcopal Church, 1915
Minot, North Dakota

First Presbyterian Church, 1915
Minot, North Dakota

A Selected List of Built & Unbuilt Commissions

First State Bank, 1915
Crosby, North Dakota

Mid-Winter Fair, 1915
Minot, North Dakota

Northwestern North Dakota Automobile
Show, 1915
Minot, North Dakota

Proj.: Second National Bank, 1915
Minot, North Dakota

Proj.: Unidentified store and office building,
1915
Minot, North Dakota

La Due Court apartment building, 1915-16
Williston, North Dakota

United States National Guard Armory, 1915-16
Williston, North Dakota

Blakey block, 1916
Minot, North Dakota

Proj.: Farmers State Bank, 1916
Grenora, North Dakota

Pearson Court apartment building, 1916
Bismarck, North Dakota

Central block (L.H. Kermott building),
1916-17
Minot, North Dakota

Eby & Young block, 1916-17
Minot, North Dakota

Proj.: Minot General Hospital, 1916-17
Minot, North Dakota

Robert B. Stacy-Judd residence, 1916-19
Minot, North Dakota

Des Lacs School, 1917
Des Lacs, North Dakota

(Proj.: Pence Automobile garage show room,
1917
Minot, North Dakota

Phil Myers residence, 1917
Minot, North Dakota

George Hager house, c. 1916-17
Minot, North Dakota

Tioga High School, c. 1916-17
Tioga, North Dakota

Ryder High School, c. 1916-17
Ryder, North Dakota,

Christian Church, c. 1916-17
Minot, North Dakota

Trolley Hospital, c. 1916-17
Trolley, North Dakota

Minot Normal School and Lincoln Park
alterations, 1917-18
Minot, North Dakota

United States Emergency Fleet Corporation,
Shipping Board Housing Div. (supervising
architect), 1918-19
Lorain, Ohio; Manitowoc, Wisconsin; and
Wyandotte, MI

Proj.: Farmers Rural Credit
Association alterations
(First Farmers Bank), 1919
Minot, North Dakota

Proj.: Kay block, 1919
Minot, North Dakota

Riverside Park Zoo alterations, 1919
Santa Monica, California

Robert B. Stacy-Judd offices, 1919
Minot, North Dakota

Proj.: Tatley-Hughes Court, 1919
Bismarck, North Dakota

1919-1922:
Edmund Taylor, Esq. residence, 1919
Calgary, Alberta
(Major and Stacy-Judd)

Proj. Unidentified residence interiors, 1919
(Major and Stacy-Judd)

Empire Hotel and commercial building
reconstruction, 1919–20
Calgary, Alberta
(Major and Stacy-Judd)

Alexander Corner alterations, 1920
Calgary, Alberta
(Major and Stacy-Judd)

Empire Theatre and apartment block, 1920
Edmonton, Alberta
(Major and Stacy-Judd)

L.R. Earl of Minto ranch house, 1920
Nanton, Alberta
(Major and Stacy-Judd)

L.R. Steel theatre, 1920
Calgary, Alberta
(Major and Stacy-Judd)

Proj.: One-Room Apartment Suites
(Copyrighted), 1920

Elbow Park Christ Church alterations, 1921
Calgary, Alberta
(Major and Stacy-Judd)

Imperial Oil Company service station, 1921
Calgary, Alberta
(Major and Stacy-Judd)

Knox United Church, 1921
Drumheller, Alberta
(Major and Stacy-Judd)

Universal Garage and Motor Company,
(also called Universal Motor Cars Limited),
1921
Calgary, Alberta
Major and Stacy-Judd

Rialto Theatre, 1921
Pasadena. Calif.

Theatre for Trans-Canada Theatres, Ltd.,
1921–22
Moose Jaw, Saskatchewan
(Major and Stacy-Judd)

Proj.: Gatti Restaurant, 1921
Calgary

Union Church, 1921
Calgary

F.L. Hammond house, c. 1921
Banff

H.H. Honans house, c. 1921
Calgary

Proj.: Canadian Battlesfield Memorial
Competition
c. 1921–22

Caley High School, c. 1921
Caley, Alberta
(Major and Stacy-Judd)

Allen Theatre, 1922
Vancouver, British Columbia
(Major and Stacy-Judd)

1922-1930:
Proj.: Unidentified residence, 1922
Santa Monica

Proj.: Beni-Hasan Theatre, Store and Office
Building, 1923–24
Arcadia

N. Bishop residence, 1923
Benmer Hills, Sparr Heights, Glendale

John Chain residence, 1923
Hollywood

Ben Hansen residence, 1923
Brentwood Heights,

Leona's Importations Building, 1923
Los Angeles

Sparr Heights theatre, bank, store, and office
building, 1923
Sparr Heights, Glendale

Worrell residence, 1923
Honolulu, Hawaii

La Granada Hotel (Hotel El Salamanca),
1923–24
Alhambra, California

Proj.: Motel O'Rodome for Hockenberry
System, 1923-24
Beaumont, California

Proj. :Beaumont Hotel, 1924
Beaumont

Krotona Institute of Theosophy, 1924
Ojai

Proj.: Laguna Beach Hotel, 1924
Laguna Beach

Proj.: Oakwood Cemetary, 1924
Chatsworth

Proj.: Unidentified hotel, 1924
Banning

Soboba Hot Springs Hotel, "The Indian
Village', 1924-27
San Jacinto

W.H. Hawkins residence, c. 1924
Glendale

The Aztec Hotel, 1924-25
Monrovia, California

Bainbridge residence, 1925
San Fernando

Norma D. Delong residence, 1925
Beverlyridge, Hollywood Hills.

Lillian Gilbert residence, 1925
Los Angeles

Proj.: Indian Center, Woodstock in the Hills,
1925
Los Angeles Co.

L.M. [or A.R.?] Keith residence, 1925
Beverly Ridge, Hollywood Hills

Kirkpatrick residence, 1925
San Fernando

Proj.: The Maya Hotel, 1925
Tijuana, Mexico

Proj.: The Maya Theatre, American Indian
Centre, 1925
Los Angeles

Merrick & Ruddick Spec housing project,
Hollywood Foothills Subdivision, 1925
North Hollywood

Adele E. Morgan residence, 1925
Beverly Ridge, Hollywood Hills

Shapely and Hunter residences, 1925
Los Angeles

W.P. Sims residence, 1925
Beverly Ridge, Hollywood Hills

Steele residence, 1925
San Fernando

Roland Stern residence, 1925
Beverly Hills

Charles Stone residence, 1925
Beverly Ridge, Hollywood Hills

George Walters residence, 1925
Beverly Hills

S.S. Woodbury residence, 1925
Beverly Ridge, Hollywood Hills

Proj.: Unidentified residence, 1925
Beverly Ridge, Hollwood Hills

Proj.: Unidentified residence, c. 1925
Beverly Ridge, Hollywood Hills

Harvey Gates residence
addition and alterations, 1926
North Hollywood

Dr. M.R. Wilcox residences, 1926
Beverly Crest, Los Angeles

Worrell residence, "The Zuni House," 1926
Santa Monica

Poltec Club, Class A Clubhouse, c. 1926
Vancouver, British Columbia

Guy D. Sisson residence, c. 1926
Hancock Park, Los Angeles

La Jolla Beach and Yacht Club, 1926-27
La Jolla

John D. Carey residence, 1927
Hollywood

Walter C. Hartman residence
addition and alterations, 1927
Beverly Hills

Los Serranos Country Club Estates, 1927
San Bernardino

William Stephenson cabin, 1927
Camp Douglas, Mina, Nevada

Twin Lakes Park tract office, 1927
Chatsworth

Proj.: World War I Memorial Tower, 1927
Minot, North Dakota

Proj.: Twin Lakes Park Model "Mayan
Home', c. 1927
Chatsworth, California

Beverly Ridge Estates, (additional site planning), 1927-28
Beverly Ridge, Hollywood Hills

H.M. Kitchell apartment building, 1928
Mount Hollywood, Hollywood Hills

First Baptist Church, 1928-32
Ventura

Neil E. Monroe residence, 1929
Sherwood Forest, Ventura Co.

Robert B. Stacy-Judd cabin, 1929
San Gabriel Mountains, Sierra Madre

Proj.: Theodore A. Willard residence, 1929;
1932
Beverly Hills

Proj.: Dr. Alderson residence, before or c.
1929
Palos Verdes

E. Bauer residences, before or c. 1929
Eaglerock

J.B. Brooks residence, before or c. 1929
Hollywood

G.E. Gardini residence, before or c. 1929
Sparr Heights, Glendale

G.C. Hall residence, before or c. 1929
Sparr Heights, Glendale

J.W. Hope residence, before or c. 1929
Los Angeles

Proj.: "Indian House", before or c. 1929
Hollywood Country Club, Hollywood

Melvin Kay residence, before or c. 1929
Annabella, Utah

R.W. Mackin residence, before or c. 1929
Morristown, New Jersey

Mr. McLean residence, before or c. 1929
Los Angeles

O.E. Rector residence, before or c. 1929
Wattles Park, Hollywood

J. Robinson residence, before or c. 1929
Santa Monica

Proj.: H.O. Shealy residence, before or c.
1929
Bainbridge, Georgia

Proj.: H.A. Snow residence, before or c. 1929
Albuquerque, New Mexico

William M. Wise residence, before or c. 1929
Pismo Beach

1930-1939

Betty Noble apartment building, 1930;
1963; 1965
Los Angeles

Dr. Gale Atwater residence, "Indian Village,"
1930-31
Elysian Park, Los Angeles

Proj.: Tatum city block (proposed), 1930-31
Wilshire District, Los Angeles

Proj.: National Hall, 1931
Hollywood

Proj.: Hancock block, 1932
Wilshire District, Los Angeles

Proj.: Ixtapalapi chapel, 1932
Ixtapalapi, Mexico

Proj.: Unidentified church, 1932
Los Angeles Co.

Proj.: Church of Jesus Christ of Latter-Day
Saints, 1934
Mexico City, Mexico

Proj.: Unidentified auditorium, 1934
Los Angeles

Murray Schloss Foundation, mgr's residence,
1935; 1960
Hollywood

Robert B. Stacy-Judd residence, 1935; 1948;
1952; 1956-57
North Hollywood

Philosophical Research Society, Inc., 1935-57
Los Angeles

Stanley Stoefen residence, 1936-37
Hollywood

Roland [or Ronald?] and Elsie Dressel
residence, 1937
Hollywood

Proj.: Henvar Rodakiewicz residence, 1937
Briarcrest, Hollywood Hills

Proj.: Roland [or Ronald?] and Elsie Dressel
ranch house, before or c. 1937
Chatsworth

Neil Monroe ranch house, before or c. 1937
San Benito

Proj.: Cafe India from the Streets of All
Nations project, 1938
Los Angeles

Harold W. Miles residence, 1938
Sunland

Proj.: Lake Mead Recreational Area,
U.S. Department of the Interior, Parks
Department,
1938-42, Colorado River, Nevada

Proj.: Boulder Beach Resort, Nevada;
Pierce's Ferry Resort, Arizona;
1938-42

Proj.: The Lost City Resort, Overton,
Nevada, 1938-42

Proj.: Boulder Beach Lodge, 1939
Colorado River, Nevada

Proj.: Detroit Leland Hotel marine hangar,
1939
Detroit, Michigan

Proj.: Guatamala City commercial hotel,
1939; 1947
Guatamala City, Guatamala

John W. Roman residence, before or c. 1939
Glendale

Dr. John Russell and Clara Twiss residence,
before or c. 1939
Hollywood

John Clark residence, c. 1939-41
Los Angeles

1940-1949

Proj.: First Baptist Church, 1940
Compton

Henry I. Harris residence, 1940-41
Glendale

Stanley G. Sachs residence, 1940-41
Glendale

Parker Mann residence, 1941
Glendale

Jon Thorbergsson residence, 1941
Elysian Heights, Los Angeles

Proj.: Enchanted Boundary resort complex,
1944-55
Los Angeles Co.

Redares residence, 1945
North Hollywood

F.J. Richmond restaurant, 1945
North Hollywood

Milton Shifman residence, 1945
North Hollywood

Barfield residence, 1945–46
Sherman Oaks

Leon Kane residence, 1945–46
Los Angeles

Douglas Cooper residence, 1946
Los Angeles

John E. Copley residence, 1946
Los Angeles

Matthew P. Fugle and Mr. and Mrs. Hall
residence, 1946
Los Angeles

Charlotte J. Johnston & Doris E. Goulding
residence, 1946
Los Angeles

YMCA and YWCA Youth Center, 1946
California

Don Conroy residence, 1946–47
North Hollywood

North Hollywood Temple Association
building (with J. Aleck Murrey), 1946–51
North Hollywood

"The American Cottage", 1948
For exhibition, Glendale

Harold Dawson residence, 1948
Palos Verdes

Morris Plan Company of California bank,
1948–49
Long Beach

Eileen Pilcher residence, 1949
Hollywood

Proj.: Set designs for the film "The Scarlet
Empress," 1949
Hollywood

1950-1959

F.D. Steadman residence, 1950
Canoga Park

Proj.: H.A. and E.M. Zerold apartments,
1950
Jackson, Wyoming

Proj.: Aseguradora-El Quetzal Hotel, 1951
Guatemala City, Guatemala

Proj.: Family Bomb Shelter, 1951
Eilene Gibson residence, 1951
Hollywood

Erich W. Korngold residence, 1951
North Hollywood

Proj.: Christian University, Chapman
College, c. 1951
North Hollywood

J. Bruce Renick residence, 1952
North Hollywood

Harold Summers residence, 1952
Sunland

San Fernando Valley Home Show,
"The Architect's Cottage," 1952–53
Burbank

Hesby Street School, 1952–53
(with W. H. Hillier) Encino

Proj.: North Hollywood Maternity and
General Hospitals, 1952–57
North Hollywood

Morris Brown residence and apartments,
1953
Van Nuys, California

Morris Brown residence, 1954
Sherman Oaks, California

Proj.: Hospital for Dr. M.M. Davidson, 1954
Van Nuys

Proj.: Orchard Gables Sanitorium and
Hospital, 1954-58
Hollywood

Benny Szladowski residence, 1955
Lancaster

Proj.: Linda Brody residence, 1956
San Fernando Valley

Proj.: Institute of Religious Science Church,
1957
Palm Springs

Spencer Howard residence, 1958
North Hollywood

Proj.: Dr. Bernard Jensen's Hidden Valley
Health Ranch, 1958
Escondido

C.A. Chapin apartment building, 1958-59
North Hollywood

B.P. Helferich residence, 1959
Sunland

Proj.: Glen Rishes drive-in restaurant, 1959
San Fernando Valley

Proj.: World University for Roundtable, Inc.,
1959
Los Angeles County

1960-1965

Howard Hampton fallout shelter, 1961
Sherman Oaks

Porj.: Church for Harold Shields, 1961
Monterey

Lou Stratford residence, 1961; 1966-67
Hollywood

Builders Exchange exhibition, 1962
Los Angeles

Leo B. Eylar residence, 1962
Studio City

Proj.: Church of Religious Science, 1963
North Hollywood

Richard Dee Halvorson residence, 1963
North Hollywood

Proj.: Leslie Ford Rest Home, 1963-67
North Hollywood

Proj.: Henry Pinczower residence, 1964
Los Angeles

Proj.: Valley Doctors Hospital, 1964
North Hollywood

Donn L. Ingram residence, 1964-65
Malibu

A Selection of Published and Unpublished Writings
by Robert Stacy-Judd

Humours of House Furnishing in the Stone Age. London: Messrs. W. Jelks and Sons, 1905.

Humours of the History of Personal Adornment (Ancient and Modern). Westcliff, England: T. J. Johnson, 1905. Drawings also appeared in The Southend Echo in 1905: October 11 and 18; November 1, 22, and 29; and 1906: January 3, 17, and 24; February 7 and 21; March 7 and 21; April 11 and 18.

Gems from ye Magic Toy Cave: R. Prentice, His Notes. Eastbourne: R. Prentice of ye Alexandra Library, 1909.

Stroud and His Son: Their Book. Tunbridge Wells: H.P. Stroud & Son, c. 1909.

Short story: "Carden Reece," published in (Editor), *Short Story Time Table* (Tunbridge Wells), April 10, 1909, n.p.

(Editor), *Eastbourne and Sussex Society* Journal (1909–10).

"Well!" *Ventnor Advertiser,* July 1911, n.p.

"A Lost Soul: A Suggestion," *Ventor Advertiser,* July 19, 1911, n.p.

"Mad! Or the Story of Ambition's Penalty," *Ventnor Advertiser,* December 30, 1911, n.p.

"My First Airplane Flight," (unpublished) c. 1911.

A Study in Black and White. (a play). Ventnor: privately published, 1911.

"Candid Criticisms," *Ventnor Advertiser,* month unknown, 1912, n.p.

The Pierrot's Dream. (a play, performed February 4, 1913 at the Town Hall, Ventnor, Isle of Wight). Ventnor: privately published, 1912.

Drachla. (a play, later renamed "Murg"; first performed December 17–19, 1914, at the Grand Opera House, Minot, North Dakota. Directed by H.J. Linney, performed by The Lynman Players). Minot, North Dakota: Privately published, 1914.

A Zero Weather Doggeral. (a poem). Minot, North Dakota: privately published, Winter, 1915.

"Birthday Greetings to C.F. Watson, Waseca, Minn.," 1916 (unpublished poem).

"The Mint House, Pevensey, Sussex," *Western Architect,* 24, July, 1916: 103–106.

Tales From Old Timers. Minot, North Dakota: privately published, c. 1917.

"The Trails of the Pioneer Architect," *Western Architect,* 26, December, 1917: 46.

"In Wartime," (published in a newspaper, probably in Minot, North Dakota), May, 1918.

The Jovial Ghost. Minot, North Dakota: privately published, 1919.

Robert B. Stacy-Judd published a series of short poems under the pseudonym Y. Minot: *"Alone,"* published January 2, 1919 and *"Work, Damn You, Work!"* published 1919 in an unknown newspaper. He refers to them as "boosters," written at the request of the editor.

Selections of the Architectural Works of Major and Stacy-Judd, Architects and Engineers. Calgary and Edmonton: privately published, 1920.

"Beverlyridge: An Ideal Hillside Development Known As 'The Last of the Best of Beverly Hills'," *California Home Owner* 3, May, 1925: 20–21, 30.

Bibliography

"Construction Lessons of Santa Barbara Quake Reviewed by Los Angeles Architect," *Southwest Builder and Contractor,* August 28, 1925: 43-44.

"The Santa Barbara Earthquake: A True Story," (unpublished), 1925.

"The Spanish Farmhouse Type of Architure for Krotona Institute of Theosophy," *The Architect and Engineer,* 88, November, 1925: 62-72.

"Maya or Aztec Architecture," *The Architect & Engineer* 85, May, 1926: 55-64.

"Reviving Maya Architecture," *The New York Times,* January 30, 1927: Sec. 2: 8.

"To An Architect," (a poem), *Pencil Points 8,* December, 8, 1927: 764.

Robert B. Stacy-Judd, Architect and Engineer. (no publisher or place is indicated), c. 1927.

"The Maya Race," (a poem) *Pencil Points, 10,* April, 1929: 277.

"Maya Architecture," *Pacific Coast Architect,* 30, November, 1926: 26-31.

The Architect's Cost and Profit. (editor), Hollywood: Architects' League of Hollywood, 1926.

Mayan Architecture—Its Adaptability to Modern Conditions: A Lecture in Three Parts, Delivered Before the Architects' League of Hollywood. Los Angeles: Southwest Builder and Contractor, 1927.

La Jolla Beach and Yacht Club, La Jolla, California, (no publisher or place indicated).

"Move for True American Architecture Growing," *Los Angeles Times,* August 20, 1933, pp. 21, 23.

"Why the Mayas Would Not Use a Wheel," *Los Angeles Times Sunday Magazine,* November 26, 1933, pp. 4-5.

"Wanted: An All-American Architecture with Ancient Mayan Motifs as a Background," Part I, *The Architect and Engineer,* 115, October, 1933: 10-19.

"Mayan Art and the Classics," Part II, *The Architect and Engineer,* 115, November, 1933: 33-40.

"An All-American Architecture," Part III, *The Architect and Engineer,* 11, December, 1933: 29-36.

"An All-American Architecture," Part IV, *The Architect and Engineer,* 30, January, 1934: 29-38.

"Some Local Examples of Mayan Adaptations," *The Architect and Engineer,* 30 (February 1934): 21-30.

The Ancient Mayas: Adventures in the Jungles of Yucatan. Los Angeles: Haskell-Travers, Inc., Publishers, 1935.

"Maya Architecture: Architect-Explorer Replies to Critic," *The Architect and Engineer,* 124, February, 1936: 19-23.

Atlantis: Mother of Empires. Los Angeles: De Vorss & Co., Publishers, 1939.

"The Maya Race," *Poets on Parade,* 1939.

"Going Back to Atlantis," (in collaboration with Sam Bagby), *Los Angeles Times Magazine,* February 25, 1940: pp. 7-8.

A Maya Manuscript (Codex Merida). Los Angeles: Philosophical Research Society, 1940.

"Through Central American Jungles," *Hughes News,* 5, August 18, 1944: n.p.

"Perilous Adventure in The Canadian Far North," *House-Warven's Center of Light,* February, 1951: 14.

"Is the Wheel a Boon to Man—or a Curse?" *House-Warven's Center of Light,* March, 1951: 23.

"Does Crime Pay?" *House Warven's Center of Light,* April, 1951: 22.

"Jungle Adventure," *House-Warven's Center of Light,* May, 1951: 18.

"The Outcast," *House-Warven's Center of Light,* June, 1951: 19.

"The Mint House," *House-Warven's Center of Light,* July, 1951: 9-10.

"Atlantis, Mother of Empires," *House-Warven's Center of Light,* September, 1951: 20-21.

"Human Document No. 1," *House-Warven's Center of Light,* October, 1951: 4.

"The Fireplace," *House-Warven's Center of Light,* November, 1951: 9.

"Doorway to the World," *House-Warven's Center of Light,* December, 1951: 13.

"Afraid of Fear," *House-Warven's Center of Light,* date unknown, c. 1951: 5.

"Manana," *House-Warven's Center of Light,* date unknown, c. 1951: 3.

Kabah: Adventures in the Jungles of Yucatan. Hollywood: House-Warven, Publishers, 1951.

"Human Document No. 2," *House-Warven's Center of Light,* January, 1952: 3.

"The Curse" *House-Warven's Center of Light,* February, 1952: 20.

"The Curse," (2), *House-Warven's Center of Light,* March, 1952: 19.

"The Earth Beneath," *House-Warven's Center of Light,* April, 1952: 12.

"The Outcast," *Gusto, 3,* no. 7, October, 1952: 41-44.

Death of A Butterfly, as Broadcast by the Distinguished Stage Star Guy Bates Post. Hollywood: House-Warven, Publishers, n.d.

Atlantis: Mother of Empires. (2d Edition). Los Angeles: De Vorss & Co., Publishers, 1979.

A Selection of Writings About, and Illustrations of the Work of Robert B. Stacy-Judd.

"Major and Stacy-Judd, Arch., Empire Hotel, Edmonton, Alberta," *Western Architect 31,* December, 1921: 13-14.

"Aztec Breathes of Olden Days," *Pacific Coast Record, 16,* October, 1925: 5-10.

Barnard, A.L. "Aztec Hotel is Modernization of Mayan Architecture," *The Western Hotel Reporter,* 42: 2, January, 1926: 8-10.

Blades, Leslie Burton. "Maya Architecture and a Modern Architect," *The Home Builder,* 4, May, 1926: 6-8, 26.

"An Adaptation of Mayan Architecture," *Architecture and Building,* 58, June, 1926: 122-124.

"California Homes," *The Home Builder,* 4, July, 1926: 33, 40, 43, 47.

"The Aztec Hotel of Monrovia, California," *The Hotel Monthly,* 34, no. 401 August, 1926: 60-64.

"California Homes," *The Home Builder,* September, 1926: 11.

Edgar, N.H. "Designing and Operating a Hotel That Will Appeal to Tourists," *Hotel Management,* 10, October, 1926: 296-300.

"Maya Influence in Southern California Decorating," *Good Furniture,* 27, October, 1926: 181-182.

"Maya Architecture," *American Architect,* 131, January 5, 1927: 7-10.

"Reviving Mayan Architecture," *The New York Times Magazine,* January 30, 1927: Sec. 2:8..

Hampton, Edgar Lloyd. "Rebirth of Prehistoric American Art," *Current History,* 25: 5, February, 1927: 624-634.

Barnard, A.L. "Architect Diagnoses Hotel Trouble," *The Western Hotel Reporter,* 44:12, March, 1927: 26.

Hampton, Edgar Lloyd. "American Architecture First: Californians Apply Ancient Mayan Motif to Modern Practical Structures," *Los Angeles Times,* April 24, 1927: 1-2.

Harkins, N.M. "Reviving the Wonders of Maya Kings," *Popular Mechanics,* July 1927: 76-78.

Minster, Joe. "Soboba Indian Village," *Pacific Coast Record,* 18, July 1927: 5-9.

Newcomb, Rexford. "Aboriginal American Architectural Types," *The Western Architect,* 36, July, 1927: 106-113.

Newcomb, Rexford The Spanish House for America. Philadelphia: J. B. Lippincott Company, 1927: 16-17, 39-40, 47, 103

Hampton, Edgar Lloyd. "Los Angeles," *Overland Monthly and Out West Magazine,* August, 1927: 229-231, 252.

Editors of the Western Architect, "Comments" on a review by Rexford Newcomb of George Oakley Totten's Maya Architecture. *Western Architect,* 36, July, 1927: 116.

Hampton, Edgar Lloyd. "Art in Industry: An American Culture Ten Thousand Years Old," *The Industrial Digest,* September, 1927: 18, 52, 61.

Hampton, Edgar Lloyd. "In Aboriginal Homes We Now Can Live," *The New York Times Magazine,* October 30, 1927: 12, 21.

Stevenson, Collier. "Spain Inspired These Bungalows," *Pictorial Review (New York),* November, 1927: 6.

"Modern House With Indian Atmosphere," *Arts and Decoration,* 28, November, 1927: 76, 108.

"American Home Built like a Moroccan Riad," *Arts and Decoration,* 74, December, 1927: 74.

"How to Have Your Hotel's 'Story' Told in Pictures," *Hotel Management,* January, 1928: 18-19.

Hampton, Edward Lloyd. "Creating a New World Architecture," *Southern California Business,* April, 1928: 16-17, 38, 45, 48.

"Norman English Design for Los Angeles Home of Charm," *Arts and Decoration,* 28, April, 1928: 75.

Stevenson, Collier. "The Ever-Colorful Spanish Design: A Popular Adaptation to Suit Our Sunnier Regions," *Pictorial Review (New York),* April, 1928: n.p.

M.J.O. "Arquitectura Azteca," *Plus Ultra (Buenos Aires),* 13, no. 145, May, 1928: n.p.

"Ancient Mayan Motifs in New Architecture," *The Christian Science Monitor,* May 9, 1928: 6.

Hampton, Edgar Lloyd. "Digging Up Ancient America," *Overland Monthly,* December, 1928: 411-412, 414.

Das Bunte Blatt (Stuttgart) 7, February, 1929: 152.

"Zabawki Miljarderow," *Swiatowid (Czechoslovakia)* 12, February, 1929: n.p.

Lewis, Jack. "Mayans to Guide Architect: Stacy-Judd to Study Old Ruins for New Ideas," *Hollywood Reporter,* February 4, 1930: 2.

Picturesque Monrovia. Monrovia, California: Charles F. Davis, 1929.

"The Well of Human Sacrifice," *Los Angeles Evening Herald,* April 29, 1930: 3.

"Mayan Culture," *Los Angeles Times,* June 5, 1930: n.p.

"Mayans to Guide Architect," *Hollywood Citizen,* Feb. 4, 1930: n.p.

"Architect Studies Works of the Mayas in the Jungles of Yucatan," *Southwest Builder and Contractor,* June 27, 1930: 32-34.

"Los Angeles Architect's Pictures of Two Notable Ruins of the Mayans," *Southwest Builder and Contractor,* September 5, 1930: 34-35.

"Robert Stacy-Judd, Arch., Indian Village, Soboba Springs," *Western Architect,* 40, February, 1931: ill.

Carleton M. Winslow, "The Architect's Viewpoint," *Architect and Engineer,* 104, March, 1931: 8-9.

"Quest of Mysteries in Mayan Ruins," *Los Angeles Evening Herald,* May 6, 1931: n.p.

"Tablet Tells Odessey of Mayas," *Los Angeles Evening Herald,* October 7, 1931: n.p.

"Hollywood Architect to Explore Mysteries of Mayan Pyramid," *Los Angeles Herald Examiner,* January 11, 1933; 3.

"Announcing a Series of Articles on Mayan Architecture," *The Architect and Engineer,* 114, September, 1933: 41-42.

Onderdonk, Jr.,Francis S. The Ferro-Concrete Style. *New York: Architectural Book Publishing Co., Inc,* 1928: 98-100.

"Mayan Architecture Evolved from Huts Adapted for Modern Mansions," *Los Angeles Evening Herald Express,* March 26, 1934: 1.

Krammer, Gerhardt T. "Maya Design," *Architect and Engineer,* 122, September, 1935: 21-28, 41.

Slott, Jon "Theory of Atlantis Reveals Missing Link of Civilization," *Parade (Los Angeles),* 8: 45, May 5, 1936: 4-5.

"Robert B. Stacy-Judd, A.I.A.," *Town & Country Review,* 10:3, December, 1936: 55.

Slott, Jon. "The Theory of Atlantis Reveals the Missing Link of Civilization: An Interview with Robert B. Stacy-Judd," *Southern California Parade,* 8:45, May 5, 1936: 4-5.

"Mayan Expert At Hughes Plant," *Hughes News,* 4:2, December 10, 1943: 3.

"Robert B. Stacy-Judd, A Hughes Notable," *Hughes News,* 5: 6, August 1, 1944: 3.

Interview with Robert B. Stacy-Judd. *Los Angeles Times,* November 30, 1972, sec. 4: 1.

Obituary of Robert B. Stacy-Judd. *Los Angeles Times,* February 13, 1975, sec. 3: 18.

Kinchen, David M. "Dreams That Might Have Been: Projects by Prominent Architects Were Never Built," *Los Angeles Times,* May 1, 1977, part 10: 2.

Post, Guy Bates. "The Mayas and the Language of Architecture." *Hollywood: House-Warven,* Publishers, n.d. Interview with Robert B. Stacy-Judd.

Exhibitions of the Works of Stacy-Judd

Self-curated exhibition by Robert B. Stacy-Judd of his paintings, mural designs, and pen drawings at the Association of Commerce, Minot, North Dakota, June 1914. Fifty works shown. No checklist.

Exhibition of drawings by Robert B. Stacy-Judd at the Minot Public Library, February 4–5, 1915, during the North Dakota Society of Engineers Seventh Annual Convention.

Exhibition by members of the Architects' League of Hollywood at the Regent Hotel, 6166 Hollywood Boulevard, February 8–20, 1926, including works by Robert B. Stacy-Judd.

"Architects' Building Material Exhibit," October 1926, Fifth and Figueroa Streets, Los Angeles. One of Stacy-Judd's works included in the exhibition is reproduced in the Los Angeles Times.

Exhibition director, "Architect's Home Show," Burbank Armory, 1955.

"Architectural Exhibit," Building Center, 7933 West Third Street, Los Angeles, April 15–May 15, 1962.

All-City Art Exhibition, Greek Theater, Griffith Park, n.d.

Index